Becoming a Vessel of Honor
Life After Salvation

David Erik Jones

Copyright© 2009 by David Erik Jones

Becoming a Vessel of Honor
Life after Salvation
By David Erik Jones

Printed in the United States of America

ISBN: 1-4392-4814-1
ISBN-13: 9781439248140

All rights reserved solely by the author. The author guarantees all contents are original and do not infringe upon the legal rights of any person or work. No part of this book may be reproduced in any form without the permission of the author. The views expressed in this book are not necessarily those of the publisher.

Scripture taken from the New American Standard Bible®, Copyright© 1960, 1962, 1963, 1968, 1971, 1972, 1973, 1975, 1977, 1995 By the Lockman Foundation. Used by permission.

Scripture taken from the Holy Bible, New International Version®. Copyright© 1973, 1978, 1984 by International Bible Society. Used by permission of Zondervan Publishing House. All rights reserved.

The "NIV" and "New International Version" trademarks are registered in the United States patent and Trademark Office by International Bible Society. Use of either trademark requires permission of International Bible Society.

Visit www.booksurge.com to order additional copies.

Contents

Preface iii
Holding Back 1
The Day. 5
God, I'm Still Me. 7
Running From God. 11
Life Happens. 15
Turning Point 19
Exposed 23
A Vessel of Honor. 27
Cleansing the Vessel. 31
Still Tempted. 37
Changing of the Guard 41
Building. 47
Blueprints 51
Coworker. 57
A Pyramid 61
Reinforcements. 67
Bearing Fruit. 73
The How 79
What's the Problem?. 85
Does God Discipline? 91
Fleeing and Pursuing 95
Sodom and Me 101
Pruning. 107
Cut Off 111
Samson and David. 117

Barnabas and Ananias. 123
The Bema Seat 127
Hebrews Six 133
Fearing God 141
The Promises 147
Using the Broken .151
Fruit in Keeping with Repentance 155
Tombs and Dishes 161
Integrity 165
Purposeful Living. 171
The Time Is Now 177
We Have an Enemy. 183
The Word 187
The Holy Spirit 191
The Truth About Sin 197
Deceived 203
Freedom 209
Standing in Grace 217
Living in Grace 223
The Call. 227

Preface

This book is a follow-up to *My Struggle, Your Struggle,* which chronicles my personal battle with pornography. In *My Struggle, Your Struggle* I share more insight into my long fight against sexual sin and the impact it has had on my life, my family, and my ministry. I have written *Becoming a Vessel of Honor* with less emphasis on pornography and have focused more on my life after salvation and the major awakenings which have changed me.

The truth is we all struggle with sin, whether we admit it or not. Even as Christians we face a constant inner war, a war that threatens to destroy the life God desires for us. But we have hope in Christ to change and to walk in victory and strength.

The title of this book comes from 2 Timothy 2:20-22, my life verses. They have been such a powerful part of my transformation, and I hope to share with you how they have impacted my entire life. The truths I have gained from these inspired words have helped me to see how the choices we make as Christians matters to God and how those choices directly influence our futures.

Life after salvation is not easy, though it can be victorious. God has plans for each of us, but our willingness to seek and follow Him plays a major role in the development and fulfillment of those plans. We have been given the freedom to choose how we will live as believers. That freedom is a great gift, but it can also be a dangerous thing if we misuse or abuse our liberty.

My desire for this book is that it will help you see your struggles as a Christian are not unusual and that you are not alone in your battle to live for God. I pray God will use my life and the lessons I have learned to help you find freedom, strength, joy, and peace in Jesus Christ.

Most often Christian leaders preach and teach without really helping people connect the dots. We talk about God and quote a few scriptures hoping to influence their lives, but that usually is just not enough. It is far too easy to proclaim truths from the Bible without giving practical help for those who wish for change. We spit out verses and theological terms, all the while those seeking help remain confused and hurting. I talk with people all the time who want to be transformed, but they feel helpless and alone in their battle with sin, shame, and guilt. They desire a new way to live but just don't know how to make it happen.

I have walked down the road of hopelessness and despair. I know what its like to hate myself and wish someone would change me. The pain is authentic, and the desire to be different is real, but the know-how is missing.

I want to change that, and to offer hope and help to those seeking a revolution in their lives.

This book shares a little about my own painful transformation and the events that have shaped me into the man I am today. I then reflect upon the Biblical truths and ideas that have influenced me the most. I have tried to express both the basic truths, scriptural insights, and the practical

Preface

steps that have changed me, so that others will be able to walk in victory and strength, too.

I pray you will find this book challenging, helpful, and liberating.

❈ ❈ ❈

Holding Back

For months the urge to walk to the front of the church gnawed at my soul. Every time the preacher gave an invitation, my heart begged my feet to take that first step toward the altar. But they wouldn't budge. Each time the last note of the invitational song played, I would be disappointed in myself and ashamed that I had failed to accept Jesus as my Savior. I would stand there knowing I was still unsaved. The heaviness and guilt were matched only by the relief of having not stepped out in front of everyone, which would have exposed me as someone who had a problem or need.

I knew I was hopeless without Jesus. I knew all too well the sins I had committed; the guilt and shame were unrelenting. Like everyone, I was aware of the fact I had lied, said hurtful things, stolen a few items, and had disrespected my parents, but the bigger issue for me was pornography.

My struggle with lust and sexual sin was growing rapidly; I found it more and more difficult to resist temptation. There was no doubt in my mind as to who I was inside; I hated myself, and I hated the kind of person I had become. Yet, my pride, or perhaps fear, kept me from reaching out for the help I knew I so desperately needed.

Each sermon seemed to be customized, designed specifically for me. It was as if the preacher knew way too much about me and the struggles I faced. There were many times when I wanted to shout, "Stop judging me!" But I knew he was right. I knew I needed a Savior.

At the same time, the constant message of grace and hope was encouraging, almost too good to be true. Weekly I heard about Calvary, how much God loved me, and how Jesus had died so I could be forgiven. And, I truly did want to be saved, even though I felt so unworthy and unforgivable. I understood what the preacher and my Sunday school teachers were telling me: Jesus died to pay the price for your sins, so ask Him to come into your heart.

It wasn't that I didn't get it or realize my sinfulness; I just couldn't seem to make myself give in.

When I read the Bible, it constantly pointed out that there was no way to earn forgiveness on my own or to make up for the things I had done, but every time I left the church, I felt empty and hopeless. I knew I needed Jesus, and I knew He had died for my sins, but I just couldn't make myself go forward.

I was afraid. Of what, I really don't know. Perhaps it was the fear of the unknown. Or maybe it was the constant worry about what others might think. Most likely, it was the fear of letting go and committing to a new life.

Something inside me knew that once I accepted Jesus, things would have to change. It seemed very clear to me that becoming a Christian was a serious thing, a commitment that would require a major transition in my life, and I was terrified of what that might lead to. Yes, I wanted to go to heaven, but I didn't want to let go of a few things that brought me so much pleasure. I absolutely wanted salvation, but I didn't want to have to live a boring and religious life—the kind of life I thought Christians were supposed to live, the kind of life I thought was necessary to be a real Christian.

As the months passed, I could not shake the deep-seated feeling that I needed to go forward. The desire to walk toward the altar increased, and I fought it all the way.

Most Sundays, I would tell myself that this would be the day, but when the moment arrived, I could not persuade my feet that it was the right thing to do, so I would just stand there battling within. As the pianist played the last note and the preacher closed the service in prayer, I would once again try to convince myself that next Sunday would be the day.

Looking back now, I guess I have come to realize the process is not supposed to be easy. Coming to terms with our sinfulness is not pleasant. Likewise, vowing to let go of your life and placing your soul in the hands of another is no simple thing. Also, acknowledging that not everyone is given the right to enter heaven and that some will perish in hell is difficult at best—not to mention the intellectual struggle with the thought of God becoming a man who was willing to suffer and die for me!

To confess Jesus Christ as my Lord and Savior was to put a stake down, to make a statement that I believed there was no other way to be forgiven or to gain eternal life. Doing so would bind me to the Bible and the commandments of God. I realized that salvation was more than just a ticket to heaven; it was a commitment to deny myself and to follow Jesus.

It was almost more than I could handle. I was tempted to just stop going to church altogether, but I knew that wasn't the answer. I knew what I needed to do.

❖ ❖ ❖

The Day

It was a bright, warm day. Easter was coming, and the preacher had recently spoken a lot about Jesus dying on the cross. There was a constant drumbeat within me, demanding to be heard. I struggled with it daily, wishing I could just be done with it all.

I had no excuse for resisting God. I believed He was real and that He loved me. I also believed Jesus had been born of a virgin and that He did many amazing things in His short life. There was very little doubt in my mind about the reality of His death and resurrection. In spite of it all, I just refused to make a move. In the meanwhile, my soul was in constant torment because I could not shake my bad habits. Each time I gave into temptation, I felt dirtier and became more aware of the need to change.

Finally, I came to a point of no return. I couldn't stand the thought of dying without Christ and His forgiveness any longer. It wasn't Sunday, but I couldn't wait a moment longer. I was broken.

Our preacher lived next door to the church. I walked up to his front door and rang the bell. With the simple push of a button, I was committed; there was no backing down. My heart pounded, and my palms were damp with sweat. I rang the bell again, halfway hoping no one would come to the door.

Just as I was about to turn and walk away, I heard footsteps and movement behind the big wooden door. I felt like running, and my mind raced, trying to come up with some lame excuse as to why I was there. Suddenly, the door opened wide, and I stood there, dry mouthed and unsure of what to say.

The pastor invited me in and showed me to the couch. As I walked in, somehow, the words came into my heart: I wanted to be saved.

The rest of the conversation is a blur. I am not sure exactly what I said or what the preacher said to me, but I do remember kneeling in his living room and asking Jesus to forgive me of my sins and to come into my heart. Most importantly, I felt relieved; I knew I had made the right choice. A great burden lifted off my chest, and a sense of peace rushed over me as I said my goodbyes and walked back out into the sun.

At that moment I was totally committed and ready to do whatever it took to remain faithful. I was going to give my all to Jesus because He had given all for me. I felt free for the first time in years, and I truly wanted to change my life, leaving behind all of those things that I knew were wrong. I vowed to follow Jesus wherever He led me and to do whatever He asked.

❖ ❖ ❖

God, I'm Still Me

I don't know exactly what I expected. I guess I thought everything would suddenly be different, and I would no longer want to sin. Maybe I hoped the light, free feeling I experienced would last forever.

I was soon disappointed.

The truth is my desire to sin was just as strong as it was in the days leading up to my salvation. I was confused, ashamed, and still trapped. Following Jesus was not nearly as easy as I thought it was going to be.

Questions began to crowd my mind. Why hadn't the joy and peace and good feelings lasted? If I truly loved Jesus, why did I want to sin? Was I truly saved?

Many of the things I heard in church only fueled my confusion. Well-intended lessons and comments implied that "real" Christians didn't want to sin or disobey God; only "lost" people had sinful desires; people who truly loved Jesus only wanted to do good and godly things.

The torment within continued. I convinced myself that I must not have believed enough or loved Jesus sufficiently. I often wanted to go forward when the preacher gave the invitation because I thought I needed to be saved again.

I never did. I would just sit in the pew and wonder if I had truly been saved. I knew I was sincere; I knew I had confessed my sinfulness and had asked to be forgiven. I also knew I had proclaimed Jesus as the Son of God, and I was even baptized. So, why didn't I feel different inside?

Why did I want to do the things I knew God didn't want me to do?

Those next few months were plagued by doubts. I'll bet I prayed the "Sinner's Prayer" a hundred times, just to make sure I had said it right. Each time, I hoped it would make me feel better. It didn't. I remained confused, wondering what I was doing wrong.

Looking back, I can see what the problem was: I was still me, a sixteen-year-old boy who was addicted to pornography. Even though I had been born again, I was still a young man who had been exposed to sinful things, and I continued to live exactly as I had prior to the day I knocked on the preacher's door, even though I knew it was wrong.

I don't know why I expected to suddenly feel different. I guess I had heard a few people testify about their own conversion, and some of them shared about how they had been miraculously delivered from the desire to sin. This one had been set free from alcohol and no longer wanted a drink, and that one left a druggy lifestyle the moment he was saved. I thought that was what was supposed to happen to me. When it didn't, I began to doubt whether I had been saved at all.

This is probably a very common experience, but at the time I didn't know that. I never heard anyone in church talk about their own struggles with sin. Therefore, I assumed they had all been delivered from temptation. I felt like I was the only one who couldn't get it right. I felt as if I were the only person who couldn't stop sinning enough to love Jesus the way He deserved to be loved.

It was a sobering experience. You might say it was a bit like being doused with cold water. When I asked Jesus to forgive me, I truly felt relieved and confident that I would be different. I was overwhelmed with emotion and experienced a brief time of bliss. I was joyful knowing I had been forgiven and that I was going to get to go to heaven.

But then I sinned, and sinned, and sinned. My moral failures shocked me back into reality; I was still me.

Quite frankly, I was disappointed with God and the whole salvation experience. I wanted more. I wanted to be miraculously changed in an instant. I wanted God to take away my urge to sin. When that didn't happen, I blamed God and began to question it all. Had I been duped? Was this Jesus stuff real? I wondered if I was the only person who couldn't shake loose from sin. Or maybe I really didn't love Jesus. How could I if I still wanted to sin?

After salvation my sinful nature didn't go away. The desire to sin was ever present, and my desire to give into temptation seemed to increase. As puberty took control of my mind and body, my actions grew darker and more perverse. Instead of becoming more and more Christ-like, I felt like I was becoming more and more evil. My behavior revealed a level of sinfulness I had never known before. The thirst for sexual satisfaction began to take over my life.

Where was God? Where was the joy of my salvation? Where was the help and deliverance that I had heard so much about? All I saw was the same old me.

✤ ✤ ✤

Running From God

Over the next few months, I began to grow a little cold toward Christianity. I began to notice other people who went to church seemed to do ungodly things too. Sure, I didn't think anyone was as sinful as me, but I was starting to see through the veneer of Christianity; even though everyone in church acted perfect, no one was.

I still went to church. I still had a desire to learn more about the Bible, but I also had a looming fear that God wanted more of me. Something within told me there was more to being a Christian than just going to church, praying, and occasionally reading my Bible.

I often sat in the back of the church, surrounded by my friends, watching the preacher. As I observed him, I dreaded the thought that someday I might be called to preach. That truly scared me. I just couldn't see myself in that role. Nothing about it was attractive.

Eventually, the scriptures we learned in Sunday school and the messages I heard during the worship services began to make more sense to me. A common thread seemed to run through them all: God wants you to live out the things you are reading about and being taught. It was clear. I could see it just as sure as I could see my face in a mirror. The Bible undoubtedly displayed the need to live differently from the rest of the world, not for salvation but for wholeness and peace and the favor of God.

The very idea of having to follow the commandments of God seemed unrealistic; how could He expect me to be perfect? I tried my best to reason away the constant call to learn and follow God's word. Did God *really* want me to be *good* all the time? Hadn't I already been forgiven? And who could deny that most of the Christians I knew were doing sinful things too. Besides, I was constantly reminded that we are all just a bunch of sinners anyway, and, after all, hadn't I done all God really wanted me to do? I had admitted I was a sinner, said the prayer and been baptized, and I went to church most Sundays. What more did He want from me?

I didn't want to change, not really. I liked knowing that I was going to heaven, but at the same time, I was able to do what I wanted. It was comfortable . . . kind of.

There were nagging thoughts in my mind, whispers of something more.

The torment continued. The very thought of having to stop doing the things I enjoyed was enough to make me want to avoid church, the preacher, and the Bible. By this time I had begun to drink more with my buddies, and I had begun to have premarital sex. Why was I doing these things? How could I do these things? Wasn't I a Christian? Why wasn't God changing my life? My soul cried out, "God help me or leave me alone!"

I knew I was wrong. There was no doubt in my mind that I was headed in the wrong direction, but I didn't want to stop, not yet anyway. I was having too much fun—or was I?

After getting drunk or looking at pornography or having sex, the feeling of exhilaration never lasted. Those brief moments of pleasure would end and leave me feeling terrible. I hated myself. I hated the way these things made me feel, but I couldn't seem to stop. I longed for them; something within me craved them. And, almost every time I had the opportunity to give in to temptation, I did.

I talked about my pain and confusion with Vallarie (my girlfriend at the time, who would soon become my wife). She felt the same way about some things in her life. We both knew the choices we were making were wrong. We both wanted to live differently, but we didn't know how, so we continued doing what we knew we shouldn't do because that was so much easier.

Several times we vowed to stop having sex and to live a purer life. Yet, within a week or two, we were right back in the middle of sin and right back into the guilt and shame those sins birthed into our lives. This went on right up until our marriage; we struggled with our beliefs and our desires, hoping to make better choices but seemingly unable to do so.

After we married, we stopped going to church altogether. We both knew we were saved, but church didn't fit into our schedule. I was going to college, and we were both working as many hours as we could. If we happened to be off on a Sunday, the last thing on our mind was going to church. We wanted to have fun.

We did go to the BSU (Baptist Student Union) once a week; after all, they gave us free lunches for listening to someone speak for a few minutes. Every once in a while, the speaker would touch a nerve somewhere deep in my soul. I even talked to the BSU director about what it would require to become a preacher. That didn't help me find peace because it seemed to be impossible at the time, so I buried the idea of being a minister somewhere in the recesses of my mind.

Val and I also once went to a local church, one that a couple of the regulars at the free meal had invited us to visit. We went but were not really comfortable, so we didn't go back.

❖ ❖ ❖

Life Happens

Five months into our marriage, just after Val's nineteenth birthday, we found out she was pregnant. It was a shock; this wasn't part of our big plan. What was God thinking? How could we take care of a baby? For heaven's sake, we were still just kids ourselves.

My whole world began to fall apart. I dropped out of school and took the first job I thought would quickly make me rich.

Three months later we were broke, the electricity to our apartment had been cut off, and I had a pregnant wife to care for. I was overwhelmed and confused, so I turned to the only place I knew I could: I called my mom and dad.

I can never express my gratitude for my parents and all they have done for me in my life. But their response to this moment of crisis is probably the most important thing I remember. You see, they could have belted us with a heavy dose of "we told you so", since they had recommended we wait to get married. They could have pointed out all of my failures and poor choices. They could have ridiculed and blamed, but they didn't. Instead, my parents presented us with a couple of options and then gave us the night to talk and pray about it. The next day, they helped us load up a U-Haul and moved us back home, where we lived with Val's parents until our first daughter was born.

In the meantime, I started looking for work.

I found a job through one of my best friends from high school and started working in an irrigation company's pump shop. It was a humbling and invaluable experience. My life was turning out dramatically different from what I had envisioned. All of my dreams and aspirations were evaporating before my eyes.

Life was changing rapidly, yet not everything was terrible.

One of the bright spots during that time was my effort to avoid pornography. Val and I talked about my struggle, and we decided there was no room for porn in our marriage. She was very clear about how it made her feel and what she thought about it. In an effort to please her and to avoid confrontation, I resisted temptation . . . for the most part.

As time passed, I was promoted and given some great opportunities. Within five years, I was managing a division of the small company. Along the way, we were also blessed with our second daughter.

During this time we started to sporadically attend church again, but as our family grew and my career took off and our worship attendance increased my addiction to pornography resurfaced. I had rarely looked at pornography during the first few years of my marriage. I tried desperately to honor my promise to Val to abstain from porn, and was able to fight the temptation most of the time, until I was introduced to the Internet. Once I found pornography on-line, my habit began to eat away at my resolve.

Slowly, the chains of sin began to bind me. I found myself lying to Val more often and finding more and more ways to spend a few minutes alone in front of the computer. All the while, I knew I was headed down a path of destruction. I constantly lived in fear, afraid I would be found out and my secret life would be exposed.

Our participation in church would come and go. However, at one point we became involved in a wonderful church start-up, which turned out to be a real blessing in our lives. It helped us to see there were Christians who were truly striving to live out Biblical Christianity. There was a real sense of community and very little pretense. They didn't judge us but were truly concerned for our well-being. It was refreshing and inspiring. In fact, this small group of committed and compassionate believers has probably been one of the most profound and lasting influences in my life. It was nothing fancy, but it was authentic and powerful.

Sadly, a couple of families eventually moved and others faded away and the small church disbanded. Once it did, we simply didn't look for another place to worship. As our participation in church faded so did my commitment to prayer, reading the Bible, and living in purity. As a result, I found myself more enslaved to my lustful desires.

But life seemed to be going pretty well for the Joneses. Our girls were healthy, we had moved into a nice new home, and my boss and I were talking about me eventually buying the company from him. Going to church just didn't seem to be that important anymore. We enjoyed spending our weekends at the lake or shopping or on some other adventure and gave very little thought to God or our spiritual lives. Every once in a while, we would feel guilty and attend a service or two, but seeking God was just about the furthest thing from our minds. We only went to church because we felt like we had to or that God would be mad at us if we didn't. Our hearts were not in it.

✤ ✤ ✤

Turning Point

Nothing in this world lasts forever. That is a simple fact of life.

My boss called me into his office to tell me some things had changed. In an instant, all of my well-laid plans came crashing down around me. He had sold the business, and he was giving me six months notice; I could either stay with the company in a different role, or I could move on.

The next six months passed rapidly and were full of life changing questions and decisions. What were we going to do? How was I going to find another job that paid as well as the one I had? Did we need to relocate? How were we going to pay for the house we had just purchased?

In the end, we wound up moving to Lubbock, Texas, where I took the first of several short-term jobs. None of them satisfied me; I could make decent money, but I could not fill the emptiness in my soul. Finally, after about a year, I landed a job I thought would help me establish a solid career. It seemed that our lives were back on track.

Then we got the call.

It was bedtime. Val and I had already put the girls to bed. When the phone rings at that time of night, your heart jumps into your throat, and your mind rushes with dreadful thoughts; you fear that someone you love is in trouble or has been hurt. Most of the time, those fears evaporate with the first few pleasant words from the caller. This time they didn't. It was mom, and something was wrong with dad.

Mom was calm but concerned. There was an unusual urgency in her voice that could not be mistaken. The details were sketchy: Dad was in an ambulance; there was talk about a possible tumor or blood clot; no one knew what to expect; please pray.

I was numb. Val and I sat on the bed, crying and praying for a miracle. Then we packed our bags, dropped off the girls with her parents, and drove all night to San Antonio.

When we arrived, the hospital was almost empty. It was early morning, and mom was in the waiting room virtually all alone. She told us the doctors thought dad had experienced a brain aneurysm. There were still a lot of uncertainties and lots of tests to be run. They didn't know if he would survive, and if he did, they didn't know what his life would be like.

When we were able to go in and see dad, I was overwhelmed. It was a moment that changed my life. My strong, intelligent, and active father lay before me weak and partially paralyzed. His voice was barely recognizable, and the fear in his eyes frightened me. How were we going to get through this? What was life going to look like from now on?

God has a way of turning heartache and pain into good and joyous things. For the first time in my life, I heard my dad speak of life after death and of the need to embrace what you have been given. He talked about faith and God and how much he loved us. Our family drew in, and we loved each other like never before. Dad's tragedy changed our lives.

By the grace of God, after months of rehab and with great effort on his part, dad made a full recovery.

But I did not.

Life looked different. What used to be important suddenly began to fade into the background. I had experienced an awakening. Family, God, and enjoying the blessings we had already been given began to supersede everything else in my life. My thirst for God and truth and answers to life's questions increased dramatically.

During this time, Val, the girls, and I began to attend a small church regularly. We started to get involved: we helped with Vacation Bible School, and I began to become more and more interested in studying the Bible. Within a few months, the old urge to be a minister returned, but this time I began to seriously entertain the idea. What was happening? How could I be a preacher? How could God use someone like me?

✤ ✤ ✤

Exposed

The loss of my job, my dad's illness, and our return to church were a perfect storm of events that brought me to the brink of change. I knew what I was supposed to do. I could feel it deep within; I was being called to give my life to serve God as a minister. There was no way I could deny the yearning within me. Years of running from God and ignoring Him hadn't completely extinguished the fire that smoldered in my heart, and it was begging to flame up again.

But a dark secret remained. I had not yet dealt with my struggle with pornography. I was still addicted to the rush that it offered. My struggle lurked in the dark corners of my life, and I didn't want to let it go.

No one knew who I was, not even Val. She knew I had looked at porn as a teen and earlier on in our marriage, but she was completely unaware of the depth of my addiction.

That was about to change.

As we talked about my desire to become a pastor and the impact it would have on our lives, I continued to hide my struggle. All the while, I knew I needed to modify my behavior, but I didn't know how to stop. I wanted to for the most part because I despised the way I felt about myself, and I hated the way I was deceiving Vallarie, but I was still addicted to the few moments of pleasure it offered.

We stumbled through some major decisions. We argued and fussed about our lives, our marriage, and the future we once dreamed of. We made tough choices, not sure how it would all work out.

And then, I dropped the bomb. I confessed to Val that I had been using the Internet to access porn. I poured out the hidden secrets that had been rotting me from within. I begged her for forgiveness.

It destroyed her. I had broken her heart, and our marriage was at a breaking point.

We talked and cried and yelled throughout the night. We held each other, blamed each other, and fell asleep exhausted.

As the days and weeks went by, we were able to talk more and more openly about my past and all of the shameful things I had done. I told her things no one else knew about me and shared dark secrets from my past. It was a slow and painful process that neither of us enjoyed.

Val allowed me to open up. She gave me the freedom to talk about my life and the choices I had made. She didn't judge me, but she made it clear she would not tolerate pornography in our marriage. I could finally see just how much damage I was causing by giving myself to such a terrible habit.

My dark secret was exposed, and Val loved me enough to stick with me. I was finally able to admit to God and to her who I was inside. It was a moment of painful liberation.

Our lives have not been the same since.

I eventually took a job as a part-time youth pastor at the church we had been attending. All the while, I began to work through my struggle. I searched out scriptures about sexual immorality and sin. I talked and prayed with Val, and I committed myself to purity. It became a top priority in my life. I went to war against my old habits.

Most importantly, through some incredible teaching, I began to recognize that God was willing and able to help me change. I could finally see God was not angry with me, but that He loved me despite my sinful choices; I accepted the fact that His Holy Spirit lived within me and would equip me for the fight that lay ahead.

As time passed and my relationship with God flourished, I began to believe I could actually win in my battle against lust. For the first time since my teenage years, I truly believed I could live a life free from pornography.

Our pastor began to teach us things that I had never heard before. As he taught about the Holy Spirit, salvation by grace, and freedom in Christ, my view of Christianity began to change dramatically. His lessons really empowered me and fueled my desire to know God more. It was a wonderful time of growth.

Within a year, I took a full-time position as a youth minister in a larger church. No one, other than Val and me, knew about my past. I guarded the truth and prayed no one would ever find out who I had been and all I had done. With each month that passed, I matured in my faith and remained faithful to my commitment to purity. It felt good to win in my battle against temptation. It felt even better to be able to look Val in the eye and tell her the truth. Each month that ticked by without a slip back into porn was a victory. Eventually, I was able to begin counting years of freedom.

I served the second church for two years and then took a position as the pastor of another small church. Six months later, I felt led by God to share my testimony with the congregation of our new church. It was time to open up and let others know how God had changed me and set me free. It was without a doubt one of the hardest things I have ever had to do. For the first time in my life, I publicly admitted I had a struggle with pornography.

❖ ❖ ❖

A Vessel of Honor

In the years that have passed since my first public testimony about my struggle with pornography, I have spent a great amount of time thinking about and praying about the changes in my life. Now, I feel compelled to share my story with others in hopes of helping them find ways to break free from their own struggles with sin.

As I have reflected upon my transformation, I have been able to identify some very real and powerful truths, which God has used to get my attention and change my life. Of all these truths, one stands out as the first and most influential. 2 Timothy 2:20–22 has set the tone for me and has continued to give me insight and wisdom. (All of the scripture references are taken from the New American Standard Bible unless otherwise noted.)

> In a large house there are not only gold and silver vessels, but also vessels of wood and of earthenware, and some to honor and some to dishonor. Therefore, if anyone cleanses himself from these things, he will be a vessel of honor, sanctified, useful to the Master, prepared for every good work. Now flee from youthful lusts and pursue righteousness, faith, love and peace, with those who call on the Lord from a pure heart.

This passage of scripture burst into my life as I was considering whether or not I should surrender to full-time ministry. The passion to minister was there all along, but I was uncertain about it all; I didn't know if I was ready or able to take on such an important commitment. And, I knew there were things about me and within me that were ungodly. I felt called but completely inadequate.

I guess I had never really thought about it before, but as I looked deeper into this passage, it became very evident that God does not look at all of us the same. Yes, we are all His creations, and we are all very important to God, yet the way we act and respond to Him determines a lot about our fellowship with Him and our usefulness within His kingdom.

I already knew we were all different, created with unique personalities and gifts, but I never really saw that our choices in life play such an important role in how God determines to use us. This passage clearly points out that our willingness to seek God and to avoid sin directly impacts our availability to the Lord.

This reality hit me like a ton of bricks.

For so long, I had wanted to be useful to God. I truly wanted to help others and to make a real difference in this world. However, I had never realized how much personal purity mattered and how it could prevent me from doing those good things. Yet, there it was, in scripture: the purer we are, the more useful to God we are in accomplishing the works He has created us for.

For the first time in my life, the full implication of my sins began to crash in on me. God's truth penetrated deep into my heart; His call to pure and righteous living echoed in my soul. I knew I had to change.

A new desire was birthed from those three verses: a sincere and undeniable urge to be a "vessel of honor" began to consume me. Before this, I knew God loved me, and I knew I had been adopted into His kingdom, but now I wanted more; just being saved was no longer good enough.

✤ ✤ ✤

Cleansing the Vessel

God was at work all along. His call to me and His command to be pure were unmistakable. Even as a teenager, I could see God wanted me to flee from sin. It was obvious to me that the two had to go hand-in-hand. Now, there was no doubt in my mind that God wanted to use me, but He also expected me to begin living in a new way.

The Bible teaches us that once we are born again, we are a new creation. This is seen in Colossians 3:1–10.

> Since, then, you have been raised with Christ, set your hearts on things above, where Christ is seated at the right hand of God. Set your minds on things above, not on earthly things. For you died, and your life is now hidden with Christ in God. When Christ, who is your life, appears, then you also will appear with him in glory. Put to death, therefore, whatever belongs to your earthly nature: sexual immorality, impurity, lust, evil desires and greed, which is idolatry. Because of these, the wrath of God is coming. You used to walk in these ways, in the live you once lived. But now you must rid yourselves of all such things as these: anger, rage, malice, slander, and filthy language from your lips. Do not lie to each other, since you have taken off your old self with its practices and have put on the new self, which is being renewed in knowledge in the image of its Creator. (NIV)

We also find a similar teaching in 2 Corinthians 5:17.

> Therefore if anyone is in Christ, he is a new creature; the old things passed away; behold, new things have come.

These passages have helped me to see that after I received Christ, I was a new man in His eyes. Yes, I did still act and feel the same, but that doesn't take away from the fact that something amazing had occurred within me: I was new inside; I had been born again.

This truth has been a key instrument in my transformation. For the first time, I could see that if I would follow after Him, He would help me to change and begin to live out what He had already done.

Basically, I discovered God can use "someone like me" because of who He is and what He had already done in me.

God was calling me to serve Him, and He promised to prepare me and then open doors for me to do "all kinds of good works." And that was what I wanted more than anything else in life, but it was going to require a change in my life.

His solution was written down for me: flee from lusts and pursue Him (2 Timothy 2:22). This was the formula by which I began to live my life. Nothing was off-limits. I had to examine everything in my life to see whether or not it was helping me seek God or keeping me from Him. This kind of examination is noted in 1 Thessalonians 5:21–22.

> But examine everything carefully; hold fast to that which is good; abstain from every form of evil.

Cleansing the Vessel

Purity is a choice, and it doesn't happen by accident. 2 Timothy 2:22 makes it crystal clear: we must *flee* from lusts and at the same time *pursue* godliness. The two work together in order to help us *cleanse* ourselves.

Please do not misunderstand me here; I am not at all trying to say we can somehow cleanse ourselves from all sins and save ourselves through good behavior. Salvation and the forgiveness of sins come only through faith in Jesus. I know without a doubt the Bible teaches that we cannot save ourselves or be good enough to gain eternal life, just as we see in Ephesians 2:8–10 and Titus 3:5.

> For by grace you have been saved through faith; and that not of yourselves, it is the gift of God; not as a result of works, so that no one may boast. For we are His workmanship, created in Christ Jesus for good works, which God prepared beforehand so that we would walk in them.

> He saved us, not on the basis of deeds which we have done in righteousness, but according to His mercy, by the washing of regeneration and renewing by the Holy Spirit.

So, the cleansing mentioned in 2 Timothy 2:21 must be for some other reason besides salvation. As I studied and thought about the instructions to cleanse myself, God showed me this purification was intended as an act of faithfulness and obedience to Him. He was asking me to do these things *because* I am His child, not in order to become His child. He was not demanding that I make myself pure through righteous acts, but rather that I live in purity because of the grace and love He had already shown me.

Furthermore, He revealed to me that my response to this command would determine how He was going to use me in His kingdom. In other words, my willingness to walk in purity would directly impact my role in His larger plan for mankind.

After discovering these truths and seeing how important they were, my passion for cleaning up my life kicked into high gear. The music I listened to, the television shows I watched, where I went on the Internet, and how I spent my free time all began to change. If something prompted lustful thoughts, it had to go, no matter how much I had enjoyed it in the past. This was not easy by any stretch of the imagination, but I was deeply motivated to make a difference and to change my life.

At the same time, I began to study the Bible more frequently, I started keeping a daily prayer journal, and I got my first taste of contemporary Christian music. As I rejected ungodly things, God provided God-honoring replacements.

But the most amazing thing that happened was that once I began to purposefully flee from lust and pursue righteousness, I awakened inside. I was changing from within; I was being transformed by God.

As a result of the transformation that was occurring within me, I began to pray that God would examine my heart and expose any area of my life that was not pleasing to Him. For the first time in my life, I meant it. I truly wanted God to revamp my life.

I vowed to try my best to eliminate anything that was causing me to stumble or that would prevent me from drawing closer to Him. God answered that prayer in powerful ways. In fact, many of my inner desires began to change dramatically, not because I was somehow a better person, but because I was sincere in my desire to let go of anything that was keeping me from obeying God.

Slowly, but surely, the things that used to attract me began to trouble me. The Lord opened my eyes to the truth and helped me see through the facade. Instead of seeing women as objects to be lusted over, I began to see daughters and wives and sisters—women who were loved by someone. God also helped me to see pornography as a horrible and sickening thing that causes great pain in the world: abuse, rape, broken homes, and affairs. I must admit that I was still drawn to the images and thrill of porn, but something was changing inside of me.

What used to arouse me began to create new emotions and feelings. The excitement and pleasure started to give way to a hatred of pornography and a desire to find freedom from my addiction. I thank God for this awakening. I am so grateful He allowed me to see past the images and into the pain and destruction that is left in the wake of pornography.

Likewise, I found a new desire to attend Bible studies and to worship. It seemed that every time we went to church or to a home study group, God would open up the word and pour it into my soul. I couldn't get enough.

My life was changing rapidly, and I liked it, but there was still work to do.

✤ ✤ ✤

Still Tempted

I am man. I do not want that to be an excuse, but it is reality. God created me as a sexual being, and that, thank goodness, did not change.

I will not pretend that all my temptations simply melted away. They diminished, but temptation was still there, lurking in the darkness. The new revelations and understanding helped reduce my attraction to pornography, but they did not completely wipe away its effects and appeal.

No matter how much you know something is wrong, hurtful, or immoral does not usually eliminate your desire for it. In fact knowing something is off limits can sometimes increase our cravings. It's like knowing that you shouldn't eat another donut or slice of cake, understanding you don't need it does little to diminish the longing for another bite of sweetness.

Temptation most often creeps in when you least expect it. For instance, when my family and I were watching TV and a sexually drenched commercial would come on, from out of nowhere, I would catch myself wanting to slip back into my old habits.

Boredom is also a hiding place for sin. If I was alone at home with nothing to do, I would often find myself in a battle fighting my past and the images in my mind, which threatened to kill my newfound hope. Sometimes, the battles were only short skirmishes that ended quickly, but other times, they were difficult and long-fought wars over my commitment to remain faithful and pure.

Many times I realize that I was on the verge of surrendering. My "spirit was willing, but my flesh was weak." Yet, the new understanding I had gained brought with it new power. I began to see that I was not just fighting the battles for me; it wasn't just about my own sin and purity. Instead, it was also about my family and those to whom I wanted to minister. I was now fighting for something bigger than myself.

My fear of losing God's anointing and of becoming an unfruitful Christian rallied my heart. I didn't want to throw away the chance to touch people's lives and to make a difference, all for just a few moments of empty pleasure. So, I resisted and fought like never before, digging in and stubbornly holding my ground.

I also discovered God had equipped me with new weapons. I had begun to understand that God had empowered me with the ability to withstand temptation. This amazing truth is seen in 1 Corinthians 10:13.

> No temptation has overtaken you but such as is common to man; and God is faithful, who will not allow you to be tempted beyond what you are able, but with the temptation will provide the way of escape also, so that you will be able to endure it.

The lessons from which I had only recently learned about the indwelling Holy Spirit also fueled me and helped me to rely more on prayer and scriptures. More and more, I found myself able to quote specific verses, verses that truly helped me to make wise choices. Meanwhile, other scriptures showed me God would not only help me overcome, but He would bless me for remaining faithful as well. James 1:12 points this out.

> Blessed is the man who preservers under trial; for once he has been approved, he will receive the crown of life which the Lord has promised to those who love Him.

At the same time, the songs I had started listening to on Air1 (a Contemporary Christian music station) helped me to focus on praising God. Instead of sex-saturated lyrics, I was able to listen to and sing along with songs of purity and freedom. This was such a powerful change for me.

Just as important was the fact that I was talking more and more with Val about my struggle. She listened, prayed with me, and made it clear that she loved me enough to stick with me through it all. She also opened up and told me how my past had hurt her and how my looking at pornography had made her feel ugly and inadequate as a wife. Our open and honest conversations have helped me more than she knows.

Since then, I have been able to see how stealing a few moments of pleasure was actually robbing me and my wife of true intimacy. What I thought was thrilling and exciting was destroying the most thrilling and exciting relationship God had given me. As we have worked through the pain and struggles, God has blessed us with a very deep and rich marriage. I am so grateful to both Vallarie and God for not giving up on me.

With each passing month, I found myself in a place I had never been before: I was able to withstand the onslaughts. As I learned more and changed my habits, the temptations began to become less frequent. When I was tempted, I was able to reach out for help, pray, and recall scripture. The longer I resisted and the more I sought to be truly pure, the fewer times I found myself facing ungodly choices.

Today, I seldom find myself face-to-face with temptation. I know it is still out there, but I guard the perimeter like never before. When I do become lazy or careless, I find that temptation increases. Therefore, I have learned to make sure the enemy has little access to my eyes, ears, and heart. This takes diligence and perseverance, but it is absolutely worth it.

※ ※ ※

Changing of the Guard

Our actions are determined primarily by our beliefs. Our lives are driven and protected by our values. We are guided by what we believe to be true. And, if we want to change our actions, habits and attitudes, we must change what we believe.

As my beliefs changed, the Lord began to open my eyes to new truths. These truths began to guide me into a new level of awareness. For example, I began to see that God passionately wants us to be fruitful. We often read in the Bible that God commands us, as His children, to bear good fruit for His kingdom. We can see this very clearly throughout the New Testament. Two such verses are John 15:8 and Titus 3:14.

> My Father is glorified by this, that you bear much fruit, and so prove to be My disciples.

> Our people must also learn to engage in good deeds to meet pressing needs, so that they will not be unfruitful.

When I was a young man, I could see God expected me to be different. The Bible spelled it out: to follow Christ meant to live in contrast to the world. At first, I resisted this notion. After all, who wants to be different? Besides, if I really didn't have to earn my salvation, I reasoned, then why did

I have to worry so much about personal holiness? And, after all, doesn't God love us even when we are trapped in sin?

But as I've grown in faith, matured in my knowledge of the Bible, and learned more about the character of God, I have come to see how important it is to let go of this world and reach for the promises of God.

By "living differently," I mean God wants me to have different ideals, goals, and standards by which I make choices. He wants me to have a "Christian worldview." That is to say that I need to filter my choices, desires, expectations, and relationships through the truths given to us in the Bible. As I do, I will begin to make Christ-like choices and less sinful ones.

Ultimately, one of the most important and overarching truths is the fact that God wants me to bear fruit for His kingdom. In other words, God wants me to do things that are beneficial to others and glorifying to His name.

In fact, we are told over and over again in the New Testament that we are saved for that very purpose. For example, Ephesians 2:8–10 reveals that we are saved by grace so that we can carry out good works.

> For by grace you have been saved through faith; and that not of yourselves, it is the gift of God; not as a result of works, so that no one may boast. For we are His workmanship, created in Christ Jesus for good works, which God prepared beforehand so that we would walk in them.

God does not save us just so we will go to heaven. No, He has a greater purpose for our lives. Indeed, He saves us so we will become "doers" of the word. This is seen in James 1:22–25.

> But prove yourselves doers of the word, and not merely hearers who delude themselves. For if anyone is a hearer of the word and not a doer, he is like a man who looks at his natural face in a mirror; for once he has looked at himself and gone away, he has immediately forgotten what kind of person he was. But one who looks intently at the perfect law, the law of liberty, and abides by it, not having becoming a forgetful hearer but an effectual doer, this man will be blessed in what he does.

It is when we "do" the word that we begin to bear godly fruit. So, learning to do good works is an important part of being a Christian.

On the other hand, Christians can continue to be carnal (driven by their human desires and interest). 1 Corinthians 3:1–3 shows us that immature and weak believers are still "fleshy" and are driven by the desire to satisfy human interests and passions.

> And I, brethren, could not speak to you as to spiritual men, but as to men of the flesh, as to infants in Christ. I gave you milk to drink, not solid food; for you were not yet able to receive it. Indeed, even now you are not yet able, for you are still fleshly. For since there is jealousy and strife among you, are you not fleshly, and are you not walking like mere men?

James 4:1–3 goes on to tell us that seeking to please the flesh results in sinful behavior; therefore, it results in pain and suffering and stunted spiritual growth.

> What is the source of quarrels and conflicts among you? Is it not the source of pleasures that wage war in your members? You lust and do not have; so you commit murder. You are envious and cannot obtain; so you fight and quarrel. You ask and do not receive, because you ask with wrong motives, so that you may spend it on your pleasures.

To live by the desires of our sinful nature is to bring destruction. To seek only to please ourselves is harmful, and it causes us to ignore the will and ways of God.

However, when we begin to live by faith through obedience and self-sacrifice and service to others, we begin to produce the fruit of the Spirit. Galatians 5:19–23 compares the two types of fruits side by side.

> Now the deeds of the flesh are evident, which are: immorality, impurity, sensuality, idolatry, sorcery, enmities, strife, jealousy, outburst of anger, disputes, dissensions, factions, envying, drunkenness, carousing, and things like these, which I forewarn you, just as I have forewarned you, that those who practice such things will not inherit the kingdom of God. But the fruit of the Spirit is love, joy, peace, patience, kindness, goodness, faithfulness, gentleness, self-control; against such things there is no law.

Undoubtedly, we can see the difference between godly fruit and fleshly fruit. It is very plain which one God wants to see produced in our lives.

The more I studied and explored the Bible, the more I began to see just how important good works are to God. It became very obvious to me that each Christian was saved for a reason and that God would equip them to fulfill that purpose. Philippians 2:13 tells us it is God who is at work within us to accomplish these things, and 2 Timothy 3:16 –17 show us that He has given us His word to equip us and train us for this reason as well.

> For it is God who is at work in you, both to will and to work for His good pleasure.
>
> All scripture is inspired by God and profitable for teaching, for reproof, for correction, for training in righteousness; so that the man of God may be adequate, equipped for every good work.

God has not only called us to serve Him through good works, but He has graciously equipped us for the task.

As my awareness of this truth expanded, so did my desire to do good deeds in the name of Christ. I saw it as my duty and role as a member of His kingdom. I also could see that He has promised to reward those who serve Him well.

After learning and accepting these truths, my behavior started lining up with my new system of beliefs. The awareness of God's desire for me to live in purity and good works began to guard my heart and inspire me to seek ways to avoid sin and at the same time serve others.

Finally, I could begin to see just how amazing the Christian life could be, and I wanted more!

❈ ❈ ❈

Building

As we live, we are building our lives. For those who have never received Christ as Lord, they continue to build on a weak foundation, but the one who has trusted in Jesus for forgiveness and eternal life is building upon the one and only solid foundation. Luke 6:46 –49 is commonly used to highlight this truth.

> Why do you call Me, "Lord, Lord," and do not do what I say? Everyone who comes to Me and hears My words and acts on them, I will show you whom he is like: he is like a man building a house, who dug deep and laid a foundation on the rock; and when a flood occurred, the torrent burst against that house and could not shake it, because it had been well built. But the one who has heard and has not acted accordingly, is like a man who built a house on the ground without any foundation; and the torrent burst against it and immediately it collapsed, and the ruin of that house was great.

I know most people have heard this passage of scripture. We teach that we must place our faith in Jesus if we hope to withstand the floods of life. This is true but not a complete picture. Yet, this is exactly where my knowledge had stopped before studying 1 Corinthians 3:10–15. I thought confessing my sin and asking Jesus to save me was pretty much all there was to a Christian life, but now I have a new and deeper understanding.

According to 1 Corinthians 3:10-15, becoming a Christian amounts to laying the foundation of Jesus Christ in our lives, a foundation on which the rest of our lives will be built.

> By the grace God has given me, I laid a foundation as an expert builder, and someone else is building on it. But each one should be careful how he builds. For no one can lay any foundation other than the one already laid, which is Jesus Christ. If any man builds on this foundation using gold, silver, costly stones, wood, hay or straw, his work will be shown for what it is, because the Day will bring it to light. It will be revealed with fire, and the fire will test the quality of each man's work. If what he has built survives, he will receive his reward. If it is burned up, he will suffer loss; he himself will be saved, but only as one escaping through the flames. (NIV)

When you build a house, you have to decide what kind of material you are going to use. This is a very important step and will determine a great deal about the cost, the quality, and the durability of the house. (Just ask the three little pigs!)

The Bible tells us in this passage that not only does it matter, but that our house is going to be thoroughly inspected. That's right; God is going to look at every detail of the house, testing to see what it is made of and just how well it is put together. Every house will be examined, and every nook and cranny will be closely scrutinized. In fact, God will put it to the ultimate test: fire!

I don't know about you, but once I read this and began to grasp the implications, I was shocked, scared, and ready to make some major changes in my life. Up until that point, I was not very careful about the materials and craftsmanship I was using to build upon my foundation. I was willing to skimp here and there to make life a little more comfortable or pleasurable. What was good and right was secondary to me because I had placed more value on whatever was fun, easy, or popular.

Sure, I wanted to build a house that looked well constructed. I wanted others to pass by and think, "Wow, that's a nice house; I wish mine were like that." But, I certainly didn't want anyone coming around to take a closer look, for they would have seen the many faults and shortcuts that I had taken.

The truth is I knew I had been building with shoddy material. My heart was fully aware of the fact that my works were less than godly and would not fare well if tested by fire. That's why this passage bothered me so much.

Suddenly, a passion for quality and strength began to replace my lackluster attitude toward works. I no longer wanted a fancy looking house on the outside that was ugly and poorly built on the inside; I truly wanted to start building a God honoring life, one that would not only pass inspection but would also bring pleasure to my Master and honor to His name.

God made His point and reinforced it with other passages and verses. Soon I began to seek out new building material: gold, silver, and precious stones. With this new awareness, my behavior began to change dramatically; my life began to look a whole lot better.

In the next few chapters, I want to take this idea of a building and expand it a little. The most amazing fact contained within the Bible is salvation by grace. We are saved despite our sinfulness. What this basically means is that we do not have to pour our own foundation. Instead, when we receive eternal life through faith in Christ, God freely pours out the foundation on which we will build the rest of our lives, a foundation that will never fail.

So, where do we go from there? We must construct our lives atop this foundation of grace.

❖ ❖ ❖

Blueprints

It is truly awe-inspiring when God puts things together. His timing is incredible and beyond my comprehension. I constantly need His help and intervention; otherwise, I would never change or mature in faith. I would never begin construction.

As God was revealing to me the importance of good works, He was also exposing my sinful actions. These two streams of truth eventually crossed paths and became a huge river of change, an undeniable force that continues to carry me through life.

2 Timothy 2:20–22 became the blueprint for the building that God wanted me to construct of my life. It has guided me and helped me to stay focused on the bigger picture and to strive to reach goals I have set for myself and my family. Without this passage, I doubt I would be the man I am today.

The foundation, of course, is Christ. I know I am a child of God, and I am building on the rock of salvation. No matter what else happens, the foundation will remain. This truth gives me the freedom to dream big and to work with abandon, knowing that no matter what happens, the foundation is firm and secure.

Upon that solid foundation, I have now been able to begin building the kind of life God has asked me to construct, a life of good works and purity. Both are necessary and must be joined together for structural integrity. A life of godly works cannot be built apart from living in obedience to God's commands for purity.

If I hope to do good works, then I must be committed to moral purity. In fact, God will only consistently use those who "cleanse themselves" for honorable works. If we continue to live in habitual sin and rebellion, we interfere with our usefulness to the Master builder. If we do not stick closely to the blueprints, then construction will slow down or stop altogether.

In other words, if a foreman on a worksite needs an important job done, he is going to call upon the most dependable and consistent employees, knowing they can be trusted to do the job well. There may be more gifted employees, but if they are irresponsible and less than dependable, then the foreman will use them for others jobs since he cannot count on their quality of work and commitment.

Can you see how this relates to our walk with God? If we are faithful in little things, then He will give us more assignments and responsibilities. This truth is seen in Luke 16:10.

> He who is faithful in a very little thing is faithful also in much; and he who is unrighteous in a very little thing is unrighteous also in much.

You might say He gives us more material and tools to build with when we are faithful and pure, but when we constantly seek after ungodliness, the Lord will not entrust us with the tools and task He desires to give us.

Purity of moral character matters to God! There can be no doubt about this as we read through the Bible. His standards are high, and He calls us to walk in holiness. This is what we understand as we read 1 Peter 1:13–16.

> Therefore, prepare your minds for action, keep sober in spirit, fix your hope completely on the grace to be brought to you at the revelation of Jesus Christ. As obedient children, do not be conformed to the former lusts which were yours in your ignorance, but like the Holy One who called you, be holy yourselves also in all your behavior; because it is written, "YOU SHALL BE HOLY, FOR I AM HOLY."

Can you see God truly wants us to strive for purity in our lives? We need to depend and rely on grace, but as children of God, we need to live by a different standard. If we do not, then God will call upon others to carry out His will on the earth. When this happens, we lose precious opportunities to be His hands and feet. Therefore, we miss out on joy, peace, experiencing God's amazing provisions and guidance, and we also miss out on the potential rewards.

However, if we will begin to seek Him by living in purity and integrity, we will be available and useful every time He calls upon us. As He calls and we respond, then we are able to do the good works that He saved us for. Ephesians 2:8–10 clearly teaches that God saved us for the purpose of doing good works in His name.

> For by grace you have been saved through faith; and that not of yourselves, it is the gift of God; not as a result of works, so that no one may boast. For we are His workmanship, created in Christ Jesus for good works,

which God prepared beforehand so that we would walk in them.

We are not saved *by* good works but *for* good works. Reaching heaven is not the whole purpose of our salvation; we have been saved to do good works for the kingdom of God.

But, our willingness to surrender ourselves wholly to God will impact His willingness to use us. With purity comes availability, which then opens up opportunities to serve and help others, and that produces blessings, rewards, joy, and the abundant life God truly wants us to have. James 1:12 and 2 John 1:8 reminds us of the potential rewards that God desires to pour out upon His children and how obedience plays a role in how we are blessed.

> Blessed is a man who perseveres under trial: for once he has been approved, he will receive the crown of life which the Lord has promised to those who love Him.

> Watch yourselves, that you do not lose what we have accomplished, but that you may receive a full reward.

We can also see that we have an enemy who wants to kill our hope and steal our blessings. The accuser and tempter desires to prevent us from having all that God offers us. Isn't this what John 10:10 teaches us?

> The thief comes only to steal and kill and destroy; I came that they may have life, and have it abundantly.

Grabbing hold of this truth has revolutionized my life. It has changed the way I build upon my foundation. Now, I have a passion for my own personal purity because I truly want to be a vessel of honor so God can use me to help build His kingdom. When He has an assignment, I want to be available to my King for service.

Looking back, I can see how the Bible has become the blueprint by which I am building my life. There are specific verses and passages that have inspired and instructed me, and the Lord is using them to guide me as I work with Him. I have learned to keep these verses fresh in my mind by reading them and meditating on them regularly. Doing so helps me to stay focused and determined to remain pure and available to the Lord. I believe this practice has been one of the most powerful and positive habits I have formed, and can have the same impact on anyone who is willing to take the time to seek out there own personal scriptures.

God has graciously provided us with the details we need to construct an amazing, abundant, and rewarding life. If we follow His instructions, we will find our lives beginning to take the shape that God planned all along. Just as a construction site slowly begins to take the form of a home, so our lives will begin to resemble the life of Christ.

❈ ❈ ❈

Coworker

God has not only given us the blueprints and provided us with an unshakeable foundation, He has also endowed us with a coworker, someone who will instruct us and help us build an incredible life. John 14:16–17 reminds us of this incredible truth.

> I will ask the Father, and He will give you another Helper, that He may be with you forever; that is the Spirit of truth, whom the world cannot receive, because it does not see Him or know Him, but you know Him because He abides with you and will be in you.

The Lord did not lay the foundation, give us the blueprints, and then just walk away. Instead, He works with us, helping us to build the kind of life He desires for us. 1 Corinthians 3:9 and Philippians 2:13 spell this out.

> For we are God's fellow workers; you are God's field, God's building.

> For it is God who is at work in you, both to will and to work for His good pleasure.

We are coworkers with God! He has not deserted us or left us to do all the work ourselves. Rather, He offers to help us place every board, nail, and tile of life just where they belong. After all, this is the only way we would be able to build a life that is best for us, a blessing to others, pleasing to God, and beneficial to His kingdom.

Yet, we must receive His help. God never forces Himself upon us. He is always there, waiting to act or lend a hand, but we must be willing to take Him up on His offer. We can choose to try and build our lives alone, under our own strength and with our own wisdom, or we can choose to work with God and tap into His power and knowledge.

If we choose, we can labor with God and watch as our lives change from a solid but bare foundation to an amazingly crafted structure that honors and glorifies our King.

Along the way, we will occasionally lose focus or get prideful and refuse His help. We might become lazy, overconfident or just plain careless. Every time this happens, the results are the same: a flawed piece of work that sticks out like a sore thumb, reminding us of our own imperfections and failures.

We then have to decide: will we leave our mistakes alone or ask God to help us repair them? If we are willing, He will step in and use His master skills to correct the errors. He may completely rip them out and redo the whole thing, or He might touch them up and transform what was once full of blemishes and flaws into a masterpiece. Either way, we will know it was our co-laborer's power, wisdom, and goodness that made it all possible.

That, to me, is one of the most amazing truths about God: He will take our mistakes and failures and work in them and with them. He does not drop us and turn His back on us when we error. Instead, if we will seek His grace, mercy, and forgiveness, God will use our blunders as lessons and turn evil into good. That is what God is famous for, just as we read in Genesis 50:20.

> As for you, you meant evil against me, but God meant it for good in order to bring about this present result, to preserve many people alive.

Romans 8:28 paints a similar picture as well.

> And we know that God causes all things to work together for good to those who love God, to those who are called according to His purpose.

I have experienced this countless times in my own life. For example, God has turned my pornography addiction and my struggle with sexual sin into a ministry that is impacting people around the world. The Lord has not only helped me to overcome this terrible habit, but He is now using me to make a real difference in the lives others.

Likewise, my wife and I once found ourselves in major credit card debit. After years of sacrificing, saving, and God's amazing provisions, we were able to payoff all of our creditors. Because of our poor choices and painful experience, I was compelled to ask our church to offer *Dave Ramsey's Financial Peace University* course to those in our congregation and community. We are now in the middle of our third series and dozens of families and individuals have learned how to take control of their finances.

These are just two examples of the amazing way the Lord has turned my bad choices and difficult circumstances around and used them for good. I know there are millions of people who could share similar testimonies about the grace and power of God. There is no doubt that we need God. We must rely on His help and guidance in order to build our lives in a godly way, but we also need God's grace, mercy, and goodness to correct our mistakes and failures if we hope to have a life that resembles and honors Christ.

The reality of it all is this: We do not have to work alone; we do not have to depend on our own abilities; we do not have to try and figure it all out by ourselves. God truly offers His constant help. He has given us the Holy Spirit as a Helper, but we still have to cooperate with Him and receive the help that He freely offers.

God is at work in and around us, and we are His co-workers. How we respond to Him makes all the difference. He wants to help us build an amazing life with lasting results, but we must learn to cooperate with Him. As we do, our lives will be transformed in ways we never thought possible.

❈ ❈ ❈

A Pyramid

I like to think of my life as a pyramid. The image has helped me to understand some basic biblical truths.

I recognize Jesus is the foundation on which my life is built. This foundation was laid the day I received Jesus as my Lord and Savior. Now, I am building my life on Him. This firm and secure foundation will never fail me; God has promised to never let my salvation crumble into ruins, because it is based upon the death and resurrection of Jesus Christ.

But, I am told over and over again in scripture to be careful as to how I live—as one who has been redeemed. The Bible repeatedly explains that the way I live my life truly matters to God, and I will be held accountable one day because I am a child of God. In other words, I must be careful as to how I build my life upon the foundation of Jesus.

I build upon the foundation in two ways: good works and purity. These form the framework of my life. The quality and productivity of my life depend directly upon these two areas. As I labor with God, my life begins to take shape. From the rubble of a fallen life, a life of sin and selfishness, arises new life, one that is set upon a solid foundation and erected by obedience to God and service to others.

As I build, I must be sure there is balance. If I focus too much on one area, the whole structure is put in jeopardy.

I can become too focused on obedience and find myself trapped in legalism, trying to earn God's love and condemning myself and others whenever *my rules* are not followed.

Or, I may find myself caught up with works and begin to think that God no longer cares about the way I live as long as I'm doing good deeds. This can make me numb to God's instructions about purity and moral issues.

Either way, there is a serious danger. If you build only one side of a pyramid and neglect the other, the structure will eventually fall in on itself. Likewise, if I focus too much on either obedience or works, then I find myself in danger of collapse.

Not long ago, I came across a curious passage in Ecclesiastes Chapter 7. Specifically, verses 16–18 caught my attention.

> Do not be excessively righteous and do not be overly wise. Why should you ruin yourself? Do not be excessively wicked and do not be a fool. Why should you die before your time? It is good that you grasp one thing and also not let go of the other; for the one who fears God comes forth with both of them.

The NIV puts verse 18 this way:

> It is good to grasp the one and not let go of the other. The man who fears God will avoid all extremes.

Once I read these verses, I could see God does not want me to become a Pharisee. It is not pleasing to God when I become enslaved to legalism. He does not desire that I submit myself to man-made religious "laws."

A Pyramid

Paul preached often about this very thing because the early church struggled with legalism. He addressed this issue in Galatians 3:1–3.

> You foolish Galatians, who has bewitched you, before whose eyes Jesus Christ was publicly portrayed as crucified? This is the only thing I want to find out from you: did you receive the Spirit by the works of the Law, or by hearing with faith? Are you so foolish? Having begun by the Spirit, are you now being perfected by the flesh?

He also taught Timothy to watch out for people who taught man-made religious rules and regulations as a means of sanctification. We see this in 1 Timothy 4:1–5.

> But the Spirit explicitly says that in later times some will fall away from the faith, paying attention to deceitful spirits and doctrines of demons, by means of the hypocrisy of liars seared in their own conscience as with a branding iron, men who forbid marriage and advocate abstaining from foods which God has created to be gratefully shared in by those who believe and know the truth. For everything created by God is good, and nothing is to be rejected if it is received with gratitude; for it is sanctified by means of the word of God and prayer.

You see, God knows we are sometimes extremists; we all have the tendency to occasionally go overboard. He does not want us to become fanatical about every little thing in life. Also, it is not pleasing to God when His children begin to think they can somehow earn righteousness or be holy by following their own rules and regulations.

Worse yet, we all have a tendency to place our rules upon other people. If we don't think we should say or do something or act in a certain way based on our own set of ideals, then we tend to place that opinion upon everybody. Or, we develop our own set of religious do's and don'ts and judge others by our self-righteous list.

Unfortunately, we see religious laws and extremism far too often in Christianity. For example, there are some people who believe that the King James Version of the Bible is the only authentic translation of scripture, and they look down on or reject those who believe otherwise. Also, some people are fanatic when it comes to the type of music in a church service, they refuse to accept that people are touched and drawn to God through various styles of worship, and they exalt their own preferences as the best way to praise God.

Some churches reject people who dress distinctly or who choose to cut their hair differently. We could talk about the abandonment of pregnant teenage girls, turning noses up at homeless people, or demanding that a person never have a drink of alcohol if they are going to be a "true" Christian. And, there are well meaning believers who truly think that you *must* go to church twice on Sunday and every Wednesday night if you really love Jesus.

The New Testament warns us about becoming legalistic and cautions us to be on the lookout for others who might do the same thing. These kinds of extremism are ungodly and unhealthy.

On the other hand, we should never let God's grace be an excuse for sinful living. Romans 6:1–2 boldly proclaims this truth.

> What shall we say then? Are we to continue in sin so that grace may increase? May it never be! How shall we who died to sin still live in it?

Faith in Jesus sets us free from sin and the Law of Moses. Faith in Jesus liberates us and releases the chains that once held us so tightly. This is incredible news, but we need to be careful not to let grace become a stumbling block in our lives. Grace should never be used as an excuse to sin. (We will take a closer look at these issues later in the book.)

We also need to be sure we do not become overly consumed by doing good works. Works cannot save us, and they do not sanctify us. Remember the words of Matthew 7:21-23.

> Not everyone who says to me, "Lord, Lord," will enter the kingdom of heaven, but he who does the will of My Father who is in heaven will enter. Many will say to Me on that day, "Lord, Lord, did we not prophesy in Your name, and in Your name cast out demons, and in Your name perform many miracles?" And then I will declare to them, "I never knew you; DEPART FROM ME, YOU WHO PRACTICE LAWLESSNESS."

Yes, good deeds are important, but they are not the key to salvation or sanctification. Luke 10:38–42 helps us see we need to be careful about letting good works become something other than what God intended.

Now as they were traveling along, He entered a village; and a woman named Martha welcomed Him into her home. She had a sister called Mary, who was seated at the Lord's feet, listening to His word. But Martha was distracted with all her preparations; and she came up to Him and said, "Lord, do You not care that my sister has left me to do all the serving alone? Then tell her to help me." But the Lord answered and said to her, "Martha, Martha, you are worried and bothered about so many things; but only one thing is necessary, for Mary has chosen the good part, which shall not be taken away from her."

Martha had let serving and preparing become more important than worshiping Jesus. She had become a good works martyr who believed her sacrifice was more valuable and important than her sister's adoration of the Lord. We, too, can fall into this trap if we are not careful.

Balance is needed. We need both a heart that is obedient to God and a heart that is eager to help others. If we will avoid extremes, we will be more likely to respond to the Spirit as He guides us. As a result, our lives will be transformed and reflect the power and goodness of God.

As we construct our lives upon the foundation of Jesus, we need to be cautious as to how we build so that our lives do not become one-sided or out of balance. Remember, a pyramid needs all of its sides to be equal and stable if it is going to remain strong and secure.

✤ ✤ ✤

Reinforcements

Over the past few years, God has taught me a lot more about His call to purity and good works. I now rely heavily on several Bible passages to help reinforce the truths that changed me through 2 Timothy 2:20–22. These reinforcements are like rebar: holding together the entire structure.

Titus 2:11–14 is perhaps the second most influential passage in my life. It has helped me to see just how important purity and works are in the eyes of God.

> For the grace of God has appeared, bringing salvation to all men, instructing us to deny ungodliness and worldly desires and to live sensibly, righteously and godly in the present age, looking for the blessed hope and the appearing of the glory of our great God and Savior, Christ Jesus, who gave Himself for us to redeem us from every lawless deed, and to purify for Himself a people for His own possession, zealous for good deeds.

This passage shows us that Jesus died to offer salvation to everyone, not just the Jews of His day. He died to redeem the whole world, but only those who acknowledge Him as Lord are forgiven and belong to Him. Jesus did not die to save only the people who are well behaved and pious. No, He gave His life so that no one would have to perish.

Yet, not everyone will receive Him as Lord.

Jesus died and was raised from the dead to purify for Himself a people; this is the church. (By "church" I mean all who believe in Jesus Christ. I am not specifying one denomination or only those who attend a local church regularly.)

Salvation is the entrance into the church or the "body of Christ." The Bible teaches us that those who call upon God as their heavenly Father, are instructed to make godly and wise choices, choices that will bring glory and honor and praise to His name. To do this, we must learn to tell ourselves "no" sometimes. We must learn to reject ungodly and worldly desires. And as we do, with the help of the Holy Spirit, we will mature and learn to discern the will of God. This is made apparent in Romans 12:1-2.

> Therefore I urge you, brethren, by the mercies of God, to present your bodies a living and holy sacrifice, acceptable to God, which is your spiritual service of worship. And do not be conformed to this world, but be transformed by the renewing of your mind, so that you may prove what the will of God is, that which is good and acceptable and perfect.

These verses connect our readiness to submit our desires, wants, and needs to God with the ability to discern His will. If we are unwilling to offer our bodies and minds to God then we will never grow and mature in faith and understanding. However, if we are willing to offer Him our bodies and minds, He will open our eyes and help us to see what He desires for our lives.

Likewise, we are to be a people who are zealous for good deeds. God intends for us to be people who are living out His commandment to love others! Basically, He wants us to be "doers" of the word so He can use His people to touch the lives of the lost and hurting.

Can you see how the two, godliness and good deeds, are combined? In fact, I believe if we will focus on these two things then we will fulfill the two greatest commandments given to us in Matthew 22:34–40.

> But when the Pharisees heard that Jesus had silenced the Sadducees, they gathered themselves together. One of them, a lawyer, asked Him a question, testing Him, "Teacher, which is the greatest commandment in the Law?" And He said to him, "'YOU SHALL LOVE THE LORD YOUR GOD WITH ALL YOUR HEART, AND WITH ALL YOUR SOUL, AND WITH ALL YOUR MIND.' This is the great and foremost commandment. The second is like it, 'YOU SHALL LOVE YOUR NEIGHBOR AS YOURSELF.' On these two commandments depend the whole Law and the prophets."

In this passage, Jesus tells us God mostly cares about our willingness to honor and obey Him (purity) and to love our neighbors as ourselves (works.) This is so vital. We cannot fully love and serve God without obeying Him and living in purity and holiness. John 14:15 tells us that if we love Jesus, we will obey Him.

> If you love me, you will keep my commandments.

John 15:10 adds to this truth.

> If you keep my commandments, you will abide in My love; just as I have kept my Father's commandments and abide in His love.

So, we can see that to fulfill the first and foremost commandment, we must obey God, because to obey God is to love God. This is to live in purity and righteousness. Likewise, if we want to fulfill the second greatest commandment we must meet the needs of others according to 1 John 3:16–18.

> We know love by this, that He laid down His life for us; and we ought to lay down our lives for the brethren. But whoever has the world's goods, and sees his brother in need and closes his heart against him, how does the love of God abide in him? Little children, let us not love with word or with tongue, but in deed and truth.

James 2:14–17 give us the same picture.

> What use is it, my brethren, if someone says he has faith but he has no works? Can that faith save him? If a brother or sister is without clothing and in need of daily food, and one of you says to them, "Go in peace, be warmed and be filled," and yet you do not give them what is necessary for their body, what use is that? Even so faith, if it has no works, is dead, being by itself.

Romans 13:8–10 also builds upon this truth.

> Owe nothing to anyone except to love one another; for he who loves his neighbor has fulfilled the law. For this, "YOU SHALL NOT COMMIT ADULTRY, YOU SHALL NOT MURDER, YOU SHALL NOT STEAL, YOU SHALL NOT COVET," and if there is any other commandment, it is summed up in this saying, "YOU SHALL LOVE YOUR NEIGHBOR AS YOURSELF." Love does no wrong to a neighbor; therefore love is the fulfillment of the law.

Can you see how God connects faith and love with obedience and works? This undeniable connection shows up throughout scripture, so we must realize this is extremely important to God. He has promised to save us by grace, completely and totally apart from works, but He saves us *for* good works so He will be glorified and honored as God. He purifies us by the blood of Christ and then empowers us to flee from sin and love and serve others.

That is what God desires for you and me. Salvation is not the finale. Instead, salvation is the beginning. Look again at Titus 2:11–14.

> For the grace of God has appeared, bringing salvation to all men, instructing us to deny ungodliness and worldly desires and to live sensibly, righteously and godly in the present age, looking for the blessed hope and the appearing of the glory of our great God and Savior, Christ Jesus, who gave Himself for us to redeem us from every lawless deed, and to purify for Himself a people for His own possession, zealous for good deeds.

Jesus left heaven and suffered and gave His life on the cross, not just to save us but to purify us so that He could then use us to do good deeds for other people. He died in order to build up a body of faithful followers who would continue His work.

That is our calling; every Christian should be devoted to purity and good works. Anything less misses the mark. Please do not think God is only concerned with "saving souls." Jesus died to do so much more. In fact, Matthew 28:18–20, one of our most beloved passages, makes the point well.

> And Jesus came up and spoke to them, saying, "All authority has been given to Me in heaven and on earth. Go therefore and make disciples of all the nations, baptizing them in the name of the Father and the Son and the Holy Spirit, teaching them to observe all that I commanded you; and lo, I am with you always, even to the end of the age."

The "Great Commission" is not just to go and baptize people so they will go to heaven. No, that is only the beginning. We are to disciple and teach them to obey *all* that Jesus has commanded us to do. We are to put into practice the truths that are revealed to us in the Bible.

God wants to transform and use people so they, too, can then go and repeat the process. It is what God desires for those who receive Jesus as Lord: salvation followed by a life of moral purity and loving service.

❈ ❈ ❈

Bearing Fruit

To live in purity and love is no simple thing. It requires that we learn to control ourselves and seek the well-being of others above our own desires and ambitions. Jesus never promised us Christian living would be easy; in fact, He tells us that we must deny ourselves and take up our cross if we hope to follow Him.

But, all of our sacrificial and faithful efforts are worth it. We do not labor, surrender, and seek God in vain. If that were the case, what would be the point? If God has called us to reject the pleasures of sin and self-centered living in exchange for nothing, then why would we want to follow Him?

There is so much more to the Christian life than just crossing heaven's threshold. There is the here-and-now, the life God has called us to today. There are changes to be made and work to be done. God saves us for a purpose in this life: bearing fruit.

The Bible often refers to our human lives in agricultural terms. In this case, we know 2 Corinthians 9:6 compares our works to planting seeds.

> Now this I say, he who sows sparingly will also reap sparingly, and he who sows bountifully will also reap bountifully.

Galatians 6:7–10 gives us even more to think about.

> Do not be deceived, God is not mocked; for whatever a man sows, this he will reap. For the one who sows to his own flesh will from the flesh reap corruption, but the one who sows to the Spirit will from the Spirit reap eternal life. Let us not lose heart in doing good, for in due time we will reap if we do not grow weary. So then, while we have opportunity, let us do good to all people, and especially to those who are of the household of the faith.

We can see the Bible clearly teaches that we will "reap what we sow." If we "plant" selfish, sinful, prideful, evil, and greedy deeds, we will harvest their fruits. But, if we "plant" kindness, love, service to others, giving, and obedience to God's commands, we will harvest their fruits. Which do you want? Which will result in joy and peace with God and godly rewards in this life and the life to come? Which seed does God tell you to plant?

Truly, the Lord demands we plant godly seeds so godly fruit will be produced by our lives. Titus 3:1-2, 8, and 14 highlight this truth.

> Remind them to be subject to rulers, to authorities, to be obedient, to be ready for every good deed, to malign no one, to be peaceable, gentle, showing every consideration for all men.

> This is a trustworthy statement; and concerning these things I want you to speak confidently, so that those who have believed God will be careful to engage in good deeds. These things are profitable for men.

> Our people must also learn to engage in good deeds to meet pressing needs, so that they will not be unfruitful.

The evidence is clear: God wants His children to do good deeds. He commands us to do good things for other people, to meet their pressing needs. When we do, everyone benefits and God is glorified, it is good for others and us, they are blessed and their needs are met, and we actually *profit* from living out God's command to love others as ourselves. Living this way fulfills the reasons for which we were created and saved. Plus, God blesses those who sow good deeds. It is the greatest "win-win" situation of all time. God saves us by grace, empowers and equips us for good works, and then blesses us richly when we do good deeds.

Do not be fooled; we *will* bear fruit; either man-made and artificial fruit or godly and authentic fruit, depending on which is planted in our lives. Every day we plant seeds based on the way we live. Every choice we make, every word we speak, every obedient or disobedient response to God's Word and the Holy Spirit is a seed planted. Whether we know it or not, we are indeed planting seeds daily, and we have the ability and freedom to decide which kind of seeds we sow. Matthew 6:1–4 explains it this way.

> Beware of practicing your righteousness before men to be noticed by them; otherwise you have no reward with your Father who is in heaven. So when you give to the poor, do not sound a trumpet before you, as the hypocrites do in the synagogues and in the streets, so that they may be honored by men. Truly I say to you, they have their reward in full. But when you give to the poor, do not let

your left hand know what your right hand is doing, so that your giving will be in secret; and your Father who sees what is done in secret will reward you.

This passage shows us how important it is to have godly motivation when we do good things for others. If we simply want to be recognized by people as a good and giving person then their applause is all the reward we will receive.

However, if we are truly concerned about the person in need and simply give to help them because God has asked us to do so, then we can expect our Father in heaven to see and reward us accordingly. In other words, we will gain a godly harvest; we will profit from our good deed.

John 15:8–11 gives us the same basic teaching.

My Father is glorified by this, that you bear much fruit, and so prove to be My disciples. Just as the Father has loved Me, I have also loved you; abide in My love. If you keep My commandments, you will abide in My love; just as I have kept My Father's commandments and abide in His love. These things I have spoken to you so that My joy may be in you, and that your joy may be made full.

We can once again see that God desires for those who confess Jesus as Lord to obey His commands. We can also see that God wants those who claim to be disciples to bear much fruit. When Christians bear godly fruit, they bring glory and praise to their Father in heaven. This is pleasing to God, and it fulfills the purposes of our salvation. Furthermore, we can see that doing so will produce joy!

Many Christians have no joy in their lives because they are not walking in obedience and doing good works for others. Their lives are all about their own needs and wants and based on their own desires and emotions. They seek to please only themselves and take all they can from life without regard as to how their actions are impacting others. This attitude of the heart produces discontentment, not joy.

On the other hand, when believers live in purity and serve the needs of others, they are fulfilling God's purpose and plan. This brings God glory and praise. It also gives joy to the Lord and joy to the faithful believer. When a Christian is living in harmony with God's word and Spirit, he or she will find true fulfillment and satisfaction in life. Perhaps that is why living in purity and doing good works is profitable for men!

There is no greater joy in life then doing what God has created us to do. We each have been given a gift which was given to us so that we could use it for the good of others. This is seen in 1 Peter 4:10–11.

> Each one should use whatever gift he has received to serve others, faithfully administering God's grace in its various forms. If anyone speaks, he should do it as one speaking the very words of God. If anyone serves, he should do it with the strength God provides, so that in all things God may be praised through Jesus Christ. To Him be the glory and the power forever and ever. Amen. (NIV)

God blesses us with the ability to serve Him in various ways by operating in the gifts He has given us. When we function in our gifting, we are instruments of His grace!

Furthermore, when we speak, serve, encourage, help, give, pray, mend, or whatever else we are equipped to do, we find the greatest joy and fulfillment in life-- we discover what it really means to live. Serving God may require some sacrifices and changes, but that doesn't mean we have to be miserable and unfilled.

As we serve and thus find contentment and delight, God will be glorified and exalted. This is truly what God desires to happen in the life of every person: salvation, obedient living, good works, and fulfillment of His glory and joy. That is why we are here, and when we live like that, God blesses us richly in many ways.

❊ ❊ ❊

The How

The challenge to bear fruit is real, but it is also intimidating. Also, the command to bear fruit is kind of vague; you may understand God wants us to bear fruit but be confused about what that means or how to do such a thing.

I think God has given us the answer to this perplexing question in John 15:1–17. We have already looked at the importance of bearing fruit, so I will skip to the "how to" information.

John 15:4–5 tells us we must abide in Christ if we are to bear fruit.

> Abide in Me, and I in you. As the branch cannot bear fruit of itself unless it abides in the vine, so neither can you unless you abide in Me. I am the vine, you are the branches; he who abides in me and I in him, he bears much fruit, for apart from Me you can do nothing.

John 15:10 shows us we must obey Christ's command if we are to abide in Him.

> If you keep My commandments, you will abide in My love; just as I have kept My Father's commandments and abide in His love.

John 15:12–17 reveals the command Jesus was focusing on was to love others.

> This is My commandment, that you love one another, just as I have loved you. Greater love has no one than this, that one lay down his life for his friends. You are My friends if you do what I command you. No longer do I call you slaves, for the slave does not know what his master is doing; but I have called you friends, for all things that I have heard from My Father I have made known to you. You did not choose Me but I chose you, and appointed you that you would go and bear fruit, and that your fruit would remain, so that whatever you ask of the Father in My name He may give to you. This I command you, that you love one another.

Also, Philippians 2:3–5 explains we are to love others by putting their needs and interests before our own.

> Do nothing from selfishness or empty conceit, but with humility of mind regard one another as more important than yourselves; do not merely look out for your own personal interests, but also for the interest of others. Have this attitude in yourselves which was also in Christ Jesus.

The focus of Christ's work on earth was *love*. He did not seek to please Himself or to cause harm to others for His own benefit. No, instead, Jesus considered our needs and well-being as more important than His own safety and comfort. And, He asks us to do the same thing.

Romans 13:8–10 confirms this teaching. If we love others and put their well-being and needs before our own, we will not commit sinful acts against them.

> Owe nothing to anyone except to love one another; for he who loves his neighbor has fulfilled the law. For this, "YOU SHALL NOT COMMIT ADULTRY, YOU SHALL NOT MURDER, YOU SHALL NOT STEAL, YOU SHALL NOT COVET," and if there is any other commandment, it is summed up in this saying, "YOU SHALL LOVE YOUR NEIGHBOR AS YOURSELF." Love does no wrong to a neighbor; therefore love is the fulfillment of the law.

So, if we are going to bear fruit, we must obey the command to love others. That is the simple truth. If we do good works apart from love, they amount to nothing, according to 1 Corinthians 13:1–3.

> If I speak with the tongues of men and of angels, but do not have love, I have become a noisy gong or a clanging cymbal. If I have the gift of prophecy, and know all mysteries and all knowledge; and if I have all faith, so as to remove mountains, but do not have love, I am nothing. And if I give all my possessions to feed the poor, and if I surrender my body to be burned, but do not have love, it profits me nothing.

Clearly, the Bible teaches that if we want to bear godly fruit, it cannot happen apart from loving others. We can be spiritual, pious, full of knowledge, and careful to obey man-made rules and still do nothing for the kingdom of God. However, if we will love others as Christ commands us to, we will bear much fruit.

Many times we focus way too much on religious activity and far too little on loving others. This, it appears, is exactly opposite of what Jesus wants us to do. So, instead of trying harder to be more religious, perhaps we simply need to be more loving toward others.

I believe this truth is boldly proclaimed in James 1:26–27 and 2:14–17 as well as 1 John 3:16–18.

> If anyone thinks himself to be religious, and yet does not bridle his tongue but deceives his own heart, this man's religion is worthless. Pure and undefiled religion in the sight of our God and Father is this: to visit orphans and widows in their distress, and to keep oneself unstained by the world.

> What use is it, my brethren, if someone says he has faith but has no works? Can that faith save him? If a brother or sister is without clothing and in need of daily food, and one of you says to them, "Go in peace, be warmed and be filled," and yet you do not give them what is necessary for their body, what use is it? Even so faith, if it has no works, is dead, being by itself.

> We know love by this, that He laid down His life for us; and we ought to lay down our lives for the brethren. But whoever has the world's goods, and sees his brother in need and closes his heart against him, how does the love of God abide in him? Little children, let us not love with word or with tongue, but in deed and truth.

These scriptures help us to see that it is more important to God that we love others through action and service rather than just showing up to church on Sunday mornings. Going to church is a good thing, but it should not take the place of meeting the needs of others. Likewise, prayer and Bible study are important disciplines in the life of a believer, but they should be combined with acts of love and concern for people.

Religious activities and church attendance are not supposed to be the primary goals for Biblical Christian living. In fact, scripture seems to indicate that prayer, worship, meditation, and other spiritual disciplines are primarily good and necessary because they help us become more loving and giving. God uses these religious activities to shape us and mold us, to transform us into people who live like Christ, people who bear fruit in His name.

Can you see just how important it is to love others through real and practical service? God has saved us and empowered us for the good of others, not just for our own well-being. He blesses us and gifts us so we may be able to meet other people's needs. To do so is to bear fruit; that is how true, God-pleasing religion is lived out.

I urge you to spend some time praying and thinking about whom God created you to be and how your gifts can be useful to others. You may not be a preacher, a song leader, or a Biblical scholar, but you know what, most people aren't! I assure you, you have a purpose in life. Ask God to help you see what gifts He has blessed you with and how those gifts can benefit other people.

Once God has helped you to identify your gifting, pray and ask Him to give you a supernatural love for those you are called to serve. If it is children, then request a sincere and deep love for kids. If it is the homeless, ask God to increase your awareness of their plight. If you have been called to remodel old houses for low income families, pray that He will help you to see how important the poor are to Him.

You are important and useful to the Master, and you are needed somewhere in His kingdom.

✤ ✤ ✤

What's the Problem?

As a general definition, sin is anything that violates God's holiness and goodness. Also, we could classify sin into one of two categories: that which dishonors God or that which is unloving to another person. Anything that violates Jesus' two greatest commands would be considered a sin. (Matthew 22:34-40)

Sin interferes with the fulfillment of God's glory and joy. We are told in Romans 3:23 that sin works against us in our quest to bring joy and glory to God.

> For all have sinned and fall short of the glory of God.

When we sin, we fall short of the glory of God. When we live in a way that is contrary to God's goodness, love, purity, and holiness, we are acting in opposition to the reasons we were created. Revelation 4:11 helps us to see that we are created for the purpose of God's glory.

> Worthy are You, our Lord and our God, to receive glory and honor and power; for You created all things, and because of Your will they existed, and were created.

Our very reason for existence is to live in a way that brings glory to God. When we sin, we violate that purpose. That is the first and foremost negative impact that is birthed by sin.

But, there are other problems as well. Sin not only keeps us from bringing glory to God, it also interferes with our ability to serve Him well. When we choose to live in disobedience, we choose to hinder our usefulness to the Lord. This is evident as we return to look at 2 Timothy 2:20-22.

> In a large house there are not only gold and silver vessels, but also vessels of wood and of earthenware, and some to honor and some to dishonor. Therefore, if anyone cleanses himself from these things, he will be a vessel of honor, sanctified, useful to the Master, prepared for every good work. Now flee from youthful lusts and pursue righteousness, faith, love and peace, with those who call on the Lord from a pure heart.

Do you see the connection between pure and righteous living with our ability to honor and serve God? When we are faithful and obedient, we are "vessels of honor" and are therefore available to the Master for "every good work." This truth cannot be denied.

Conversely, when we make impure and ungodly choices, we are "vessels of dishonor" and therefore have limitations placed upon our service to the Master.

Undoubtedly, God calls us to live in purity and to do good works. The two go hand-in-hand. We cannot live in immorality and rebellion and, at the same time, expect God to give us the privilege of honorable service.

Would an earthly king give a traitor access to the royal treasury? Would a general give a rebellious soldier a higher rank? Would a father give his son the keys to his business, knowing that he has been careless and unconcerned with the daily operations of the company? Likewise, do we expect God to give us blessings, authority, and responsibilities in His kingdom when we live in a way that disrespects and dishonors Him?

Serving God is the greatest of honors. It is a privilege and not a right! God saves us for service in His kingdom, but we must mature, grow, and prove ourselves faithful if we hope to gain the fullness of our salvation.

Luke 16:10–11 gives us a look into the way God sees our willingness to be faithful to Him, even in the little things.

> He who is faithful in a very little thing is faithful also in much; and he who is righteous in a very little thing is righteous also in much. Therefore if you have not been faithful in the use of unrighteous wealth, who will entrust the true riches to you.

God watches us. He tests us and observes how we handle our responsibilities, temptations, and the gifts He has entrusted to us. As He looks on, He determines how faithful, zealous, and pure we are.

When He sees a child who is faithful, He rewards him or her and gives that person more responsibilities and opportunities to do amazing things for the kingdom. When the Lord sees a child who is unfaithful, careless, and impure, God disciplines him or her and withholds the fullness of life that is available to that individual. This does not mean the child is no longer useful to the Father or that he or she is completely disqualified from service, but the child is not yet ready for what the Lord has in store for that person's life.

As you can see, the choices we make directly influence God's willingness to bless and use us. This carries with it major implications. It also shows us that the way we live our daily lives matters to God and can either lead us deeper and closer to Him or block our growth and ability to bear godly fruit.

Scripture teaches us that the Spirit will work within us and direct our paths. However, we are also told that we can quench or hinder the Spirit. This is revealed to us in Ephesians 4:30–32 and 1 Thessalonians 5:19–22.

> Do not grieve the Holy Spirit of God, by whom you were sealed for the day of redemption. Let all bitterness and wrath and anger and clamor and slander be put away from you, along with malice. Be kind to one another, tenderhearted, forgiving each other, just as God in Christ as forgiven you.

> Do not quench the Spirit; do not despise prophetic utterances. But examine everything carefully; hold fast to that which is good; abstain from every form of evil.

When we disobey God and refuse to listen to the Spirit, our hearts become hardened and we become less sensitive to His voice and guidance. This is exemplified in Ephesians 4:17–19.

> So this I say, and affirm together with the Lord, that you walk no longer just as the Gentiles also walk, in the futility of their mind, being darkened in their understanding, excluded from the life of God because of the ignorance

> that is in them, because of the hardness of their heart; and they, having become callous, have given themselves over to sensuality for the practice of every kind of impurity with greediness.

When we reject the Spirit's help and live as if we have never been taught God's word, we become more and more calloused towards the truth. Eventually, we can get to the point where we no longer even recognize His voice. In that state, we live as if our salvation doesn't matter, seeking only to please ourselves, no longer concerned for the needs and well-being of others.

So, I hope you can see that choosing to live a sinful lifestyle hinders our usefulness in the Master's hands. Also, ignoring the Holy Spirit's conviction of sin in our lives holds us back and keeps us from maturing and growing spiritually. Sin after salvation is a stumbling block that can destroy ministries, ruin marriages, squander finances, and waste the gifts that we have been given. And all of these things rob us of the joy and fulfillment that the Lord wants us to have. Therefore, we should all take our fight against sin very seriously.

❖ ❖ ❖

Does God Discipline?

I have heard it said that since Jesus died for our sins, God no longer disciplines people. This is a very nice idea, but it doesn't appear to me to be scriptural. After all, Hebrews 12:4–11 makes it very clear that God disciplines those whom He loves.

> You have not yet resisted to the point of shedding blood in your striving against sin; and you have forgotten the exhortation which is addressed to you as sons, "MY SON, DO NOT REGARD LIGHTLY THE DISCIPLINE OF THE LORD, NOR FAINT WHEN YOU ARE REPROVED BY HIM; FOR THOSE WHOM THE LORD LOVES HE DISCIPLINES, AND HE SCOURGES EVERY SON WHOM HE RECIEVES." It is for discipline that you endure; God deals with you as with sons; for what son is there whom his father does not discipline? But if you are without discipline, of which all have become partakers, then you are illegitimate children and not sons. Furthermore, we had earthly fathers to discipline us, and we respected them; shall we not much rather be subject to the Father of spirits, and live? For they disciplined us for a short time as seemed best to them, but He disciplines us for our good, so that we may share His holiness. All discipline for the moment seems not to be joyful, but sorrowful; yet to

those who have been trained by it, afterwards it yields the peaceful fruit of righteousness.

We know that love must come with correction. True love is sometimes carried out by being honest and doing what's best for the person you love, even if it causes them pain or discomfort. As this passage from Hebrews explains, parents who love their children will discipline them. Why? To help the children grow wise, to help them learn to avoid painful mistakes, and to guide them in the healthiest, safest, and most joyful direction. Discipline is good and necessary.

We have all seen the effect of parents who choose to not discipline their children. It is a sad and destructive thing. Biblically, parents who do not discipline their children are practicing a type of child abuse. The Bible tells us this very thing in Proverbs 13:24 and 19:18.

> He who withholds his rod hates his son, but he who loves him disciplines him diligently.

> Discipline your son, for in that there is hope; do not be a willing party to his death. (NIV)

If these things are true for earthly fathers, how then can they not apply for our heavenly Father who loves us much deeper and more completely? If God truly loves us, how could He not discipline us?

We truly need God to correct us when we go astray. We need Him to point out our failures and mistakes so we can learn to overcome them and avoid them in the future. We need the Lord to expose our areas of weakness and vulnerability so we will learn to act wisely and to obey His commands in the future.

Hebrews 12:11 confirms what we know to be true.

> All discipline for the moment seems not to be joyful, but sorrowful; yet to those who have been trained by it, afterwards it yields the peaceful fruit of righteousness.

Discipline hurts! Remember, when we were kids, we didn't enjoy our parent's love when it came in the form of a spanking, grounding, or some other form of discipline. But looking back, we can see that those times of discomfort helped us to make better choices and to avoid mistakes in the future.

The same is true with God. His loving hand is sometimes very firm. But it is always for our good. By God's discipline, we are trained up and we learn to discern what is good and what is evil. As God reveals our errors and failures and allows the painful consequences to impact our lives, we begin to see that God's ways are best.

I know this is true because I have experienced loving discipline from the perspective of a child and as a parent. My parents loved me enough to spank me, ground me, or punish me in some other way when I broke their rules or caused harm to someone else. They disciplined me so that I would understand what kind of behavior was acceptable and what was not. I now do the same thing for my daughters because I love them and want them to have a good future.

We are all human; therefore, we will all make mistakes and we all need to be corrected from time to time. Sin is a reality in our humanity, so we need God to help us see when we stumble into sin. When He corrects us, we need to learn from our mistake and turn from the sin.

I have personally started praying for God's discipline, not because I enjoy being disciplined, but because I know I need His loving hand to correct me and guide me into maturity, purity, and godly service. If I hope to bear much fruit, it will not happen apart from the Lord's help and the Lord's discipline.

❊ ❊ ❊

Fleeing and Pursuing

Second Timothy 2:20–22 not only contrasts honorable and dishonorable vessels, it also gives us a clear course of action to follow if we hope to bear abundant fruit in the kingdom of God.

> In a large house there are not only gold and silver vessels, but also vessels of wood and of earthenware, and some to honor and some to dishonor. Therefore, if anyone cleanses himself from these things, he will be a vessel of honor, sanctified, useful to the Master, prepared for every good work. Now flee from youthful lusts and pursue righteousness, faith, love and peace, with those who call on the Lord from a pure heart.

If we hope to be pure, we must flee from sin *and* pursue righteousness. This is what God expects and demands of those who call upon the name of Jesus. He truly cares about the way we live and instructs us to strive for purity and obedience.

I have come to realize that simply trying not to pursue sin is futile unless I begin to seek godly things in its place. To flee from sin is not enough; we need to seek after godliness at the same time if we truly want to be vessels of honor.

We have been created to pursue, and we will spend a lifetime doing so. We spend years in pursuit of an education, we strive to accomplish career goals, we spend vast amounts of time and money seeking after pleasure or fulfillment, we chase relationships, and the list goes on and on. The issue is not whether or not we will spend our life pursuing; the question is what we will pursue?

Simply stated, we must replace our search for ungodly things and selfish ambitions with godly and others-centered pursuits. When we are seeking selfish pleasure, the security of earthly wealth, the praises of men, or any other unworthy thing, we will consequently neglect the good works that God has called us to carry out. If we are focused on attaining the things of the world, then love, purity, peace, and righteousness will slip into the recesses of our minds. Our actions will most definitely follow after whatever it is we set our desires upon.

However, if we seek to please and serve God by taking care of the needs of others, then we are onto something powerful. Lust, money, thrills, and praises of men will be secondary and will, therefore, be less tempting and time consuming. This is what God wants for us. Philippians 2:3-8 spells this out wonderfully.

> Do nothing from selfish or empty conceit, but with humility of mind regard one another as more important than yourselves; do not merely look out for your own personal interest, but also for the interest of others. Have this attitude in yourselves which was also in Christ Jesus, who, although He existed in the form of God, did not regard equality with God a thing to be grasped, but emptied Himself, taking the form of a bondservant, and being made in the likeness of men. Being found in appearance

as a man, He humbled Himself by becoming obedient to the point of death, even death on a cross.

God wants us to be deeply concerned with the welfare of others. He created us to have relationships and to serve one another. Anything less is incomplete. When we are self-centered and self-serving, we miss the mark and, thereby, miss the fulfillment of life.

Jesus was willing to give everything. He laid down His life for the sake of others. That is exactly what God calls us to do: to be willing to sacrifice for the good of other people. Truly, we are most like Christ when we let go of our own interests and selfish desires, and instead seek what is best for others first.

As we do this, by the power of the Holy Spirit and a willful choice to obey the second most important command, we bring glory to God, just as Jesus did. What greater purpose is there in life? What could glorify Christ more? And, what could result in more joy?

When this is our main objective in life, sin will not be as tempting. When we are pursuing God, we tend to face less temptation *because* we are pursuing righteousness. So, to focus on godly things is a formidable weapon against temptation. Perhaps that is why God wants us to focus on the things He values and not upon the things mankind values. That is what we are taught in Philippians 4:8.

> Finally, brethren, whatever is true, whatever is honorable, whatever is right, whatever is pure, whatever is lovely, whatever is of good repute, if there is any excellence and if anything worthy of praise, dwell on these things.

Romans 12:2 points out how vital it is that we allow God to renew our minds, to change the way we think.

> And do not be conformed to this world, but be transformed by the renewing of your mind, so that you may prove what the will of God is, that which is good and acceptable and perfect.

Likewise, Ephesians 4:17-23 helps us to see the importance of setting our hearts and minds upon godly things as we try to do His will.

> So this I say, and affirm together with the Lord, that you walk no longer just as the Gentiles also walk, in the futility of their mind, being darkened in their understanding, excluded from the life of God because of the ignorance that is in them, because of the hardness of their heart; and they, having become callous, have given themselves over to sensuality for the practice of every kind of impurity with greediness. But you did not learn Christ in this way, if indeed you have heard Him and have been taught in Him, just as the truth is in Jesus, that in reference to your former manner of life, you lay aside the old self, which is being corrupted in accordance with the lust of deceit, and that you be renewed in the spirit of your mind, and put on the new self, which in the likeness of God has been created in righteousness and holiness of the truth.

There has to be an internal shift. Basically, the desires of our hearts need to be reset. We have to let the truth of God replace our old ways of thinking. He gives us a new nature, one which is created in righteousness. Now we must learn to put on the new self so that we will be able to live the way He created us to live.

Whatever our heart is set on, that is what we will live for, and we will sacrifice other things to obtain them. If it is material possessions, a place of power, or selfish pleasure, we will give up godliness and service to others so we can gain what we are seeking. However, if we are truly hungry for God and His blessings, we will begin to sacrifice and labor as needed, and we will find it much easier to make godly choices and love others.

Our inward transformation has to be a work of God, an act of grace, which He offers to everyone who has received Christ as Lord. God is constantly at work in those who have confessed Jesus as Lord, yet this amazing transformation does not happen apart from our cooperation with the Spirit. Philippians 3:12–13 highlights this truth.

> So then, my beloved, just as you have always obeyed, not as in my presence only, but now much more in my absence, work out your own salvation with fear and trembling; for it is God who is at work in you, both to will and to work for His good pleasure.

That inner calling to purity, the drawing from within, that thirst for goodness, love, and peace, and the whisper that tries to help you make the right choice are in fact God. He is planting holy desires and righteous thoughts within you, but you must choose to surrender your will and submit to His leadership; that is the part we play in our transformation and sanctification.

God is working! That we know, but we should not expect Him to force us to change. Instead, God asks us to give our hearts and minds to Him willfully by following wherever He leads and by doing whatever He prompts us to do.

As we work with God by living in purity and good works, we are expressing our love and devotion to Him. The Bible teaches us that fleeing from sin and meeting the needs of others is, in fact, loving God, and as we abide in love, we bear fruit. It all fits together.

We cannot bear godly fruit when we are seeking after sin. If we want to produce the fruit of the kingdom of God, then we must replace our pursuit of sin with a pursuit of righteousness, faith, love, and peace. It is all about the deepest desires of the heart.

Furthermore, seeking after sin always leaves one empty, ashamed, and longing for more, while seeking God brings the greatest joy and fulfillment. A life spent seeking after God is truly worth it. The more we understand this, the more we are transformed.

❖ ❖ ❖

Sodom and Me

I don't guess I would have ever equated my life with those who lived in Sodom and Gomorrah. I would have written them off as the worst of the worst, far more immoral and impure than me, but as I have studied the scriptures, I have found a shocking similarity in my own lifestyle and theirs.

As a matter of fact, I have always thought of the Sodomites as nothing more than extremely sexually immoral pagans. Now, I see they are eerily similar to me and the rest of our modern society. Ezekiel 16:48–50 helps me to see just how close we are.

> "As I live," declares the Lord God, "Sodom, your sister and her daughters have not done as you and your daughters have done. Behold, this was the guilt of your sister Sodom: she and her daughters had arrogance, abundant food and careless ease, but she did not help the poor and needy. Thus they were haughty and committed abominations before me. Therefore I removed them when I saw it."

It surprised me to recognize Sodom's lack of concern for the needy, which led them to immorality. They were a rich and comfortable city. The valley around Sodom was well watered and it produced abundantly. Because of their prosperous and easy living, they become arrogant—prideful and concerned only with themselves.

The people of Sodom and Gomorrah became greedy and self-indulgent. Instead of using their prosperity for the good of others, they became lazy and absorbed in ease and pleasure. This then lead to their immorality.

God saw all of this and was not pleased; therefore, He destroyed them. God poured out His wrath because of their pride, selfishness, and immorality, and we can see from this passage of scripture just how closely they all tied in together: *selfishness led to immoral behavior.*

How does this relate to me? I see these same qualities in myself. I can be very prideful, thinking I am the reason for the prosperity and fortunate circumstances of my life.

I can also see within me a tendency to seek after the things of this world. I like stuff, comfort, and pleasure. I know I can become wrapped up in seeking my own contentment and gratification above the needs of others. This, of course, is not pleasing to God and can quickly result in sinful and selfish behavior.

I also know I can give into immorality. I have lived in immorality and know I am just one choice away from returning to that kind of lifestyle. Immorality has a certain attraction, which I cannot deny; it truly is there within me, even though I know how dangerous and destructive immoral activity can be.

The same things are true for Israel. In the passage quoted above, God is talking to the Israelites. The Lord is comparing them to Sodom. He is not pleased with His chosen people and is threatening to "cut them off." And, He eventually fulfilled this threat, according to Romans 11:17–23.

> But if some of the branches were broken off, and you, being a wild olive, were grafted in among them and became a partaker with them on the rich root of the olive tree, do not be arrogant toward the branches; but if you are arrogant, remember that it is not you who supports the root, but the root supports you. You will say then, 'Branches were broken off so that I might be grafted in.' Quite right, they were broken off for their unbelief, but you stand by your faith. Do not be conceited, but fear; for if God did not spare the natural branches, He will not spare you, either. Behold then the kindness and severity of God; to those who fell, severity, but to you, God's kindness, if you continue in His kindness; otherwise you also will be cut off.

In this passage, Paul is speaking to non-Jewish Christians. He is reminding them of God's grace, which had allowed them access to salvation through faith in Christ. But, He also warned them about becoming arrogant (prideful) and thinking they had somehow saved themselves.

Paul goes on to warn them of the possibility of being "cut off." After all, if God did not spare the Israelites, His chosen people, then how arrogant would it be to assume the gentiles would be spared if they became too prideful.

John 15:1-2 builds upon this same premise.

> I Am the true vine, and My Father is the vinedresser. Every branch in Me that does not bear fruit, He takes away; and every branch that bears fruit, He prunes so that it will bear more fruit.

In these two verses, we see the same basic warning: be careful so you will not be "taken away" or "cut off." These warnings have grabbed my attention and created a healthy fear of God within me.

I do not believe this reference to being "cut off" is referring to a person losing their salvation since that would contradict what we know to be true about salvation by grace. But, this is a real warning about God's willingness to discipline those who call upon His name. A similar warning is found in 1 Peter 1:13–19.

> Therefore, prepare your minds for action, keep sober in spirit, fix your hope completely on the grace to be brought to you at the revelation of Jesus Christ. As obedient Children, do not be conformed to the former lusts which were yours in your ignorance, but like the Holy One who called you, be holy yourselves also in all your behavior; because it is written, "YOU SHALL BE HOLY, FOR I AM HOLY." If you address as Father the One who impartially judges according to each one's works, conduct yourselves in fear during the time of your stay on earth; knowing that you were not redeemed with perishable things like silver or gold from your futile way of life inherited from your forefathers, but with precious blood, as of a lamb unblemished and spotless, the blood of Christ.

The truth is clear: God wants us to live in a pure and loving way after we place our faith in Jesus Christ as our Lord and Savior. Salvation does not negate the command to flee from lust and to pursue righteousness, peace, and love. No, in fact, as born again children of God, we should be zealous for purity and good works, and God will hold us accountable as to the way we live as believers.

If we become arrogant or too comfortable with life, we may find ourselves knee- deep in sin. Remember, our behavior is always driven by our deepest desires and our deepest beliefs. If we want to live godly lives, we must make sure our desires and beliefs are driven by the things of God.

The Lord takes this very seriously. He did not spare Sodom and Gomorrah or Israel. Do we really believe that He will spare us if we live in opposition to Him?

❈ ❈ ❈

Pruning

If we hope to become vessels of honor, we must understand that at times the process will be painful. If we want to bear fruit for the kingdom of God, we need to know there will be times when God is going to test us to expose areas of weakness and need in our lives. Let's look again at John 15:1–2.

> I Am the true vine, and My Father is the vinedresser. Every branch in Me that does not bear fruit, He takes away; and every branch that bears fruit, He prunes so that it will bear more fruit.

God is in control. He is watching and knows us inside and out. He is working with each of us in order to accomplish His purpose and will. This process is not easy or pain free for those who belong to Him.

If we are children of God, then we can expect the Father to chastise us and deal with areas of weakness and failure. This means there are times when our relationship with God will be strained and painful. It also means God will get our attention, correct us, and do whatever is required to help us mature and grow to completion. Hebrews 12:7 explains this well.

> It is for discipline that you endure; God deals with you as with sons; for what son is there whom his father does not discipline?

God knows what's best. He knows what He wants to accomplish through us and in us, and this requires discipline. He loves His children enough to not give up on us or to leave us as we are.

This process is painful but is absolutely for our best interest. It also makes us more useful in the kingdom, and it ultimately produces more fruit for the kingdom of God. Hebrews 12:10–11 reminds us of the benefits of discipline.

> For they (our earthly fathers) disciplined us for a short time as seemed best to them, but He disciplines us for our good, so that we may share in His holiness. All discipline for the moment seems not to be joyful, but sorrowful; yet to those who have been trained by it, afterwards it yields the peaceful fruit of righteousness.

As we can see in this passage, God corrects us for our good, so we can bear more fruit for His kingdom. He fully intends for us to become more and more righteous in our actions and fruitful in our deeds. Truly, this is God's will for all who have received Jesus as Lord.

The process is like pruning a plant. The plant will not reach its full potential unless it is occasionally trimmed back. As withering and dying branches are cut away, new and healthy branches take their place, bearing more fruit.

As children, we have a choice to make. We can either cooperate with God by listening, learning, and making wise choices once God corrects us, or we can rebel and flee toward ungodliness. How we respond will make all the difference in our growth, our fruitfulness, and our reward.

If we hope to be vessels of honor, we need to learn from our mistakes and mature in our faith when God corrects us.

Pruning is not always discipline. Sometimes God allows trials to come into our lives to help mature us spiritually, to build us up in the faith. This is exactly what we see in Romans 5:1–5.

> Therefore, having been justified by faith, we have peace with God through our Lord Jesus Christ, through whom also we have obtained our introduction by faith into this grace in which we stand; and we exult in hope of the glory of God. And not only this, but we also exult in our tribulations, knowing that tribulation brings about perseverance; and perseverance proven character; and prove character, hope; and hope does not disappoint, because the love of God has been poured out within our hearts through the Holy Spirit who was given to us.

God will allow us to face trials and hardships because they train us up as children of God. We sometimes need difficulties and challenges to build our character, so God uses tribulations to accomplish this in us.

Pruning is a necessary process if we hope to grow and mature spiritually. Without it, we will remain infants in Christ and never be able to bear abundant fruit. This is exemplified in 1 Corinthians 3:1–3 and Hebrews 5:12–14.

> And I, brethren, could not speak to you as to spiritual men, but as to men of flesh, as to infants in Christ. I gave you milk to drink, not solid food; for you were not yet able to receive it. Indeed, even now you are not yet able, for you are still fleshly. For since there is jealousy and strife among you, are you not fleshly, and are you not walking like mere men?
>
> For though by this time you ought to be teachers, you have need again for someone to teach you the elementary principles of the oracles of God, and you have come to need milk and not solid food. For everyone who partakes only of milk is not accustomed to the word of righteousness, for he is an infant. But solid food is for the mature, who because of practice have their senses trained to discern good and evil.

God loves us enough not to leave us in infancy. He will help us along, correcting us, and allowing trials and hardships to mature us. This causes us to grow spiritually, bear more fruit, and experience the greatest amount of joy in life.

❖ ❖ ❖

Cut Off

As I was studying through John Chapter 15, my eyes were opened to a reality that I had never seen before. Right there in the middle of this beautiful image of being connected to Jesus, I found a couple of very threatening and intimidating verses. John 15:1–2 screamed for my attention.

> I Am the true vine, and My Father is the vinedresser. Every branch in Me that does not bear fruit, He takes away; and every branch that bears fruit, He prunes so that it will bear more fruit.

The NIV reads like this:

> I am the true vine, and my Father is the gardener. He cuts off every branch in me that bears no fruit, while every branch that does bear fruit he prunes so that it will be even more fruitful.

I struggled with, prayed over, and studied for hours upon this passage. I was on a journey to see what John meant when he wrote that those who are "in Christ" could be "cut off" or "taken away."

As I searched through scripture, I found more and more information about this subject, and God began to clarify the picture, bringing me a new and deeper understanding. The first of these collaborating verses was Romans 11:17–24.

In this passage, Paul wrote about Israel and how God had fulfilled His promise to break them off when they refused to seek and obey Him. Paul then related this to the gentiles who were saved by grace.

> But if some of the branches were broken off, and you, being a wild olive, were grafted in among them and became partaker with them of the rich root of the olive tree, do not be arrogant toward the branches; but if you are arrogant, remember that it is not you who supports the root, but the root supports you. You will say then, "Branches were broken off so that I might be grafted in." Quite right, they were broken off for their unbelief, but stand by your faith. Do not be conceited, but fear; for if God did not spare the natural branches, He will not spare you, either. Behold then the kindness and severity of God; to those who fell, severity, but to you, God's kindness, if you continue in His kindness; otherwise you also will be cut off.

This passage nearly knocked me over. The picture is very clear: God disciplined the Israelites for their unbelief, as it was displayed by their rebellious and immoral actions. Then, Paul warns the Christians not to become arrogant by thinking they are beyond the same discipline of God.

The term used here in Romans was the same as in John: cut off. This is serious business, so we must find more evidence to help us understand what God wants us to know.

I looked back at John Chapter 15 and found verses 4–6.

> Abide in Me, and I in you. As the branch cannot bear fruit of itself unless it abides in the vine, so neither can you unless you abide in Me. I am the vine, you are the branches; he who abides in Me and I in him, he bears much fruit, for apart from Me you can do nothing. If anyone does not abide in Me, he is thrown away as a branch and dries up; and they gather them, and cast them into the fire and they are burned.

If we hope to find truth, the truth that can set us free, we need to come to terms with this passage. It is, after all, God's holy word, and therefore, we cannot afford to simply ignore it or reject it altogether when it makes us uncomfortable.

Clearly, Jesus is teaching that if Christians hope to bear fruit, they can do so only by abiding in Him. To understand this passage, we need to understand what the word "abide" means. According to *Strong's Compete Dictionary of the Bible*, abide means to stay or remain.

So how does a person "remain" in Christ? The answer is found in John 15:10.

> If you keep my commandments, you will abide in My love; just as I have kept My Father's commandments and abide in His love.

Could this be any clearer? If we hope to "abide in Christ," it will not come about other than by obeying His commands. If we refuse to obey by pursuing ungodliness, lust, the love of money, or other sinful things, then we are living apart from Christ, and in that state, we cannot produce godly fruit because we are no longer abiding in Him.

Now, please understand, once again, I am not at all teaching that a person can lose his or her salvation. I believe there is more than enough scriptural evidence to absolutely conclude that once individuals sincerely believe in their hearts and confess with their mouths that Jesus is the Christ, they are saved and sealed by the Holy Spirit. We are saved by grace alone by placing our faith in Jesus. Our ability or inability to avoid sin and do good works does not secure eternal life. Eternal life is given to those who receive Jesus as Lord, not to those who are able to obey the Law!

However, this does not mean a person who believes in Jesus always "abides" in Christ, for a Christian can choose to submit to God or to their flesh. If you don't believe this, then just read Romans Chapters 6, 7, and 8. Paul himself dealt with the struggle of sin and submitting to God.

The fact is Christians can choose to disobey God. Christians can decide to give into temptation. Abiding in Christ is a choice. It is also the key to bearing God-pleasing and God-glorifying fruit, which in turn, is the key to joy. John 15:11 sums it up this way.

> These things I have spoken to you so that My joy may be in you, and that your joy may be made full.

Christians can experience the full, joyful, and abundant life that God promises but only if they choose to live in obedience to God's commands, which then opens up the opportunity to bear much fruit. If they chose to live in another way, they run the risk of being "cut off." This is a serious warning.

Once I began to dig into John 15, I had to have more answers; I had to know more about the potential consequences of a Christian living apart from Christ. As I explored the Bible and prayed, God's word opened up and poured out more and more evidence that convinced me that I was on to something life changing. 1 Corinthians 5:1–6 is one example, and it spoke volumes.

> It is actually reported that there is immorality among you, and immorality of such a kind as does not exist even among the Gentiles, that someone has his father's wife. You have become arrogant and have not mourned instead, so that the one who had done this deed would be removed from your midst. For I, on my part, though absent in body but present in spirit, have already judged him who has so committed this, as though I were present. In the name of the Lord Jesus, when you are assembled, and I with you in spirit, with the power of our Lord Jesus, I have decided to deliver such a one to Satan for the destruction of his flesh, so that his spirit may be saved in the day of the Lord Jesus.

There is no ambiguity here. Paul boldly stated that a Christian, who was a member of the church at Corinth, was sleeping with his father's wife. This was without a doubt immoral. Paul condemned this sinful lifestyle and demanded that the Corinthians take action.

He then pointed out they had become arrogant or proud (NIV) or puffed up (KJV) about the matter. Is this the same kind of arrogance that we read about in Romans 11: 17 –24 where Paul teaches us not to be prideful about our salvation by grace and not works?

It seems to me Paul is confronting the Corinthians about their pride in being saved, and they had not addressed the issue because they didn't feel it was that big of a deal since the man was already forgiven. They boasted of their position in Christ, they boasted of their spiritual gifts, and they boasted of being saved by grace. Yet, they would not deal honestly with the sin in their midst.

Paul rebuked the church for their unwillingness to address the issue. He then instructed them to remove the man who was living in a sinful lifestyle. Paul ordered the local church to remove this man from their congregation and to no longer associate with him. You could say Paul was telling them to cut him off!

Was this man going to lose his salvation? No, absolutely not. Verse 5 puts that notion to rest immediately. The man was certainly going to face some real and severe consequences (being turned over to Satan and the destruction of his flesh), but he was still going to be saved.

This brings me both fear and relief. I can see in this short passage the dire warning to obey God and to flee from sin, but I can also see the certainty of my salvation in Christ.

If I fall into sin, I may be cut off, but God will not strip away my salvation. After all, I was not saved by doing good or avoiding sin; I was saved by placing my faith in Jesus.

✣ ✣ ✣

Samson and David

King David and Samson were two men who were called by God for a special purpose, and in these two men, we can see how God responds to sin and repentance. Samson was "cut off," but David repented and continued to bear fruit; you might say he was pruned. There is no doubt from scripture that both of these men were chosen by God to do amazing things. (Judges 13 spells this out for Samson, and 1 Samuel 16 details how God instructed Samuel to anoint David as the new king of Israel. Both were chosen by God and given works to fulfill.)

If both of these men were called into service by God, what separated them in their usefulness to God? Can we identify one as a man of honor and one as a man of dishonor?

You may have never thought about it before, but both David and Samson had a lust problem. King David, as you probably already know, fell into adultery and murder. 2 Samuel 11:15 gives us a brief look into his terrible mistake.

> Then it happened in the spring, at the time when kings go to battle, then David sent Joab and his servants with him and all Israel, and they destroyed the sons of Ammon and besieged Rabbah. But David stayed at Jerusalem. Now when evening came David arose from his bed and walked around on the roof of the king's house, and from the roof he saw a woman bathing; and the woman was

> very beautiful in appearance. So David sent and inquired about the woman. And one said, "Is this not Bathsheba, the daughter of Eliam, the wife of Uriah the Hittite?" David sent messengers and took her, and when she came to him, he lay with her; and when she purified herself from her uncleanness, she returned to her house. The woman conceived; and she sent and told David, and said, "I am pregnant."

David messed up big time! He had an affair with the wife of one of his "mighty men." He then plotted to have his loyal soldier killed in battle to try and cover up his sin.

But God saw it all and was not pleased. Soon after, God sent a prophet to confront David, to give him a chance to repent. Second Samuel 12:13-14 show us how David responded and how that impacted his fellowship with God.

> Then David said to Nathan, "I have sinned against the Lord." And Nathan said to David, "The Lord also has taken away your sin; you shall not die. However, because by this deed you have given occasion to the enemies of the Lord to blaspheme, the child also that is born to you shall surely die."

David did repent and God forgave him. However, because of David's sins, God disciplined him. The discipline even spilled over upon his family; that was the consequence of David's willingness to dishonor God by committing adultery and murder.

But, because he repented, David was still useful to God. His reign was tainted, and he faced hardships and heartaches for the rest of his life due to his sinful choices, but God forgave him and continued to use the king in honorable ways.

Samson is well known for his superhuman powers which were given to him by God. Those powers came with extra responsibility and a specific command to never cut his hair; doing so would result in the Lord removing Samson's strength and protection.

Samson grew up and developed a taste for forbidden women. He constantly frolicked with them and did not uphold the high standards given to him by God. Judges 16:1 gives us a brief glimpse into the life of Samson.

> Now Samson went to Gaza and saw a harlot there, and went in to her.

This one verse pretty much sums up the life-long struggle of Samson. We know this choice and many others that he made were not pleasing or honorable to God.

Time after time, Samson acted recklessly and barely escaped the enemy with God's help, and yet he did not learn from his mistakes. We never read of Samson repenting. He apparently never showed remorse but only anger and pride, and He continued in his immoral ways. Eventually, God removed His hand of protection, and Samson paid the price. Judges 16:18–21 tells us what happened to Samson.

> When Delilah saw that he had told her all that was in his heart, she sent and called the lords of the Philistines, saying, "Come up once more, for he has told me all that is in his heart." Then the lords of the Philistines came up

to her and brought the money in their hands. She made him sleep on her knees, and called for a man and had him shave off the seven locks of his hair. Then she began to afflict him, and his strength left him. She said, "The Philistines are upon you, Samson!" And he awoke from his sleep and said, "I will go out as at other times and shake myself free," But he did not know that the Lord had departed from him. Then the Philistines seized him and gouged out his eyes; and they brought him down to Gaza and bound him with bronze chains, and he was a grinder in the prison.

Samson's pride and careless living finally caught up with him. God removed His special anointing from Samson's life because Samson refused to live in purity and he disobeyed the Lord's specific command concerning his hair.

Samson then faced humiliation and a very dishonorable death. This powerful, blessed man of God was blinded and bound by the enemy and turned into a means of entertainment to the Philistines. They mocked the Lord and sacrificed to their god thinking that it had delivered Samson into their hands.

Samson had become a vessel of dishonor.

Yes, God still used him to bring about a victory for Israel, but only after Samson cried out to God and offered to give his life to defeat the enemy. His life ended in ruins!

I wonder how Samson's story might have turned out had he lived faithfully. What if he had repented and sought to live a pure and God honoring life? What if he had used the strength God had given him for the purpose of delivering Israel? Would he have died as a chained and blinded prisoner underneath a pile of rubble?

As we look at the lives of David and Samson, we can see some similarities. We see they were each called by God, and we notice they both acted immorally. What separates them is David's willingness to repent and Samson's stubborn pursuit of sin. Today, which is revered with honor, and which is used as an example of folly? Which would we say was used for honorable works, and which died in dishonor?

❈ ❈ ❈

Barnabas and Ananias

You may be tempted to think the accounts of David and Samson are just one-time events, something God would not carry out today. You may believe that since David and Samson lived under the Old Testament Laws and not under grace, God would handle things differently now.

Well, I want to give you more scriptural evidence of the validity of this warning. Acts 4:32–5:6 is one such example.

> All the believers were one in heart and mind. No one claimed that any of his possessions was his own, but they shared everything they had. With great power the apostles continued to testify to the resurrection of the Lord Jesus, and much grace was upon them all. There were no needy persons among them. For from time to time those who owned lands or houses sold them, brought the money from the sales and put it at the apostles' feet, and it was distributed to anyone as he had need. Joseph, a Levite from Cyprus, whom the apostles called Barnabas (which means Son of Encouragement), sold a field he owned and brought the money and put it at the apostles' feet. Now a man named Ananias, together with his wife Sapphira, also a piece of property. With his wife's full knowledge he kept back part of the money for himself, but brought the rest and put it at the apostle's feet. Then Peter said, "Ananias, how is it that Satan has so filled your heart that you have lied to the Holy Spirit and have

kept for yourself some of the money you received for the land? Didn't it belong to you before it was sold? And after it was sold, wasn't the money at your disposal? What made you think of doing such a thing? You have not lied to men but to God." When Ananias heard this, he fell down and died. And great fear seized all who heard what had happened. Then the young men came forward, wrapped up his body, and carried him out and buried him. (NIV)

This passage gives us a clear example of a man who was an "honorable vessel" and one who was not.

Barnabas (Joseph) was not seeking the praises of men and was sincerely looking out for the needs of others. This, according to James 1:26–27, is pure and undefiled religion in the sight of God. Therefore, God used Him in a mighty way, and this passage honors his sacrifice.

This is the same Barnabas whom we read more about in other parts of the Bible. He served with Paul and did other great works.

Ananias, on the other hand, was more interested in the praises of men and wealth. He and his wife plotted together to *appear* to do a good work. They schemed and lied in order to show others that they were good people and obedient Christians. The action was good, but the motivation of their heart was not.

God was not pleased! They were not living by the Spirit; instead, they were living by the flesh. Their hearts were set on financial gain and praises of men. Their primary concern was not meeting the needs of others. Acts 5:7–8 reveals their true motivation.

About three hours later his wife came in, not knowing what had happened. Peter asked her, "Tell me, is this the price you and Ananias got for the land?" "Yes," she said, "that is the price." (NIV)

From these verses, we can see that Ananias and his wife knew they were lying, and they plotted to make the apostles believe they had given to the church all of the proceeds of the sale of their land. The couple was putting on a show and trying to look as if they were generous. They acted in an ungodly way, and in this case, God's judgment was quick. He knew their hearts and "cut them off" immediately.

Like me, you may be overwhelmed with questions about this passage. Until recently, I had a very limited understanding of this difficult story. Why did God do this? How could God kill two people who professed faith in Christ? After all, they were members of the church, and they were giving some money to the poor. Wasn't that good enough? How could a loving God do such a thing?

But, now, after gaining more knowledge of the truth and praying about this and similar passages, I have come to a new and fuller understanding.

Ananias and Sapphira were perfect examples of vessels of dishonor. I do believe they were Christians, just as the man in 1 Corinthians 5 was a Christian. Yet, they chose to disobey God. They were greedy and thirsted after money and the praises of men rather than sincere obedience and service.

They were still Children of God, even though they acted sinfully, but instead of using them for honorable things, as God did with Barnabas, He used them for dishonorable service. What was their service? They became an example. Their death caused others, believers and non-believers alike, to fear God. We can see this in Acts 5:9–11.

> Peter said to her, "How could you agree to test the Spirit of the Lord? Look! The feet of the men who buried your husband are at the door, and they will carry you out also." At that moment she fell down at his feet and died. Then the young men came in and, finding her dead, carried her out and buried her beside her husband. Great fear seized the whole church and all who heard about these events. (NIV)

Their sin led to an untimely death; they were cut off prematurely and in a very dishonorable way. In fact, even today, we look at them and shake our heads, wondering what they were thinking.

I do believe that had they resisted temptation, God would have used them and blessed them in some other way. Or, if they would have repented when confronted by Peter, God would have shown them grace and restored them. But, they did neither and reaped the harvest of what they sowed, and have since become known as vessels of dishonor.

❈ ❈ ❈

The Bema Seat

There are some things we learn in life that change us, lessons that have an overwhelming impact and influence us for the rest of our lives. Learning about the "Bema Seat" has had that kind of impact on me.

I, like so many other Christians, was completely unaware of the Bema Seat. I was almost thirty years old before I ever even heard about the "Judgment Seat of Christ". I had been taught about the "Great White Throne Judgment" in which the unbelievers are judged and cast into the eternal lake of fire, but no one had ever taught me about the judgment of Christians.

The Bema Seat is mentioned in Romans 14:10 and 2 Corinthians 5:10.

> But you, why do you judge your brother? Or you again, why do you regard your brother with contempt? For we will all stand before the judgment seat of God.

> For we must all appear before the judgment seat of Christ, so that each one may be recompensed for his deeds in the body, according to what he has done, whether good or bad.

The Greek word used to describe the seat of authority by which people were judged during the times of Christ was *Bema* (bay'-ma). This was a platform or raised area where a person in authority would sit and judge those who were brought before him. That is the word that is translated as the judgment seat in many passages, including Matthew 27:19.

> While he was sitting on the judgment seat, his wife sent him a message, saying, "Have nothing to do with that righteous Man; for last night I suffered greatly in a dream because of Him."

In this verse, Pontius Pilate was sitting in his place of authority and Jesus was brought before him by the Jews. Pilate's wife had a nightmare about Jesus and warned Pilate not to have anything to do with Him.

This same word, Bema, is used elsewhere in scripture, too. Acts 18:12 gives us another look at this place of judgment.

> But while Gallio was proconsul of Achaia, the Jews with one accord rose up against Paul and brought him before the judgment seat...

So, we can see the Bema, which is translated in most modern versions of the Bible as "judgment seat," was a place where people were brought before an authority so judgment could be passed.

This same word is used to describe the place in which every Christian will be judged based on their works. This is seen clearly in 2 Corinthians 5:6–10.

> Therefore, being always of good courage, and knowing that while we are at home in the body we are absent from the Lord—for we walk by faith, not by sight- we are of good courage, I say, and prefer rather to be absent from the body and to be at home with the Lord. Therefore we also have as our ambition, whether at home or absent, to be pleasing to Him. For we must all appear before the judgment seat of Christ, so that each one may be recompensed for his deeds in the body, according to what he has done, whether good or bad.

There can be no doubt Paul is describing the judgment of those who believe in Christ. The context of the passage is clear: Paul is writing to people who have placed their hope and faith in Jesus as their Lord and Savior; otherwise, they would have no hope and could not look forward to being at home with the Lord.

This judgment does not determine one's salvation, for that has already been determined by placing one's faith in Christ. Also, this judgment has nothing to do with the judgment of sins, because all of our sins have already been forgiven once and for all! God will remember our sins no more, just as He has promised.

The judgment seat of Christ is strictly a judgment of works. All Christians will give an accounting of the works they have done as children of God. This truth is seen in 1 Peter 1:17–19.

> If you address as Father the One who impartially judges according to each one's work, conduct yourselves in fear during the time of your stay on earth; knowing that you

were not redeemed with perishable things like silver and gold form your futile way of life inherited from your forefathers, but with precious blood, as of a lamb unblemished and spotless, the blood of Christ.

The teaching is very clear in this passage that Christians will be judged based upon their works. Again, this judgment will not determine salvation, since all Christians have already been cleansed of all of their sins and given eternal life by placing their faith in Jesus' death and resurrection.

The judgment, however, will determine the rewards each believer will receive. This is taught to us in 1 Corinthians 3:10–15.

By the grace God has given me, I laid a foundation as an expert builder, and someone else is building on it. But each one should be careful how he builds. For no one can lay any foundation other than the one already laid, which is Jesus Christ. If any man builds on this foundation using gold, silver, costly stones, wood, hay or straw, his work will be shown for what it is, because the Day will bring it to light. It will be revealed with fire, and the fire will test the quality of each man's work. If what he has built survives, he will receive his reward. If it is burned up, he will suffer loss; he himself will be saved, but only as one escaping through the flames. (NIV)

Once we have received Jesus as Lord, our foundation is set and will never crumble, but the life we live after salvation will determine our heavenly rewards. The works we do for the good of others and the glory of God will be richly rewarded. However, the works that are selfishly motivated or opposed to God's purposes and goodness will be consumed, and we will suffer the loss of our heavenly rewards.

Every Christian will be held accountable at the Bema Seat. We will give an accounting of our lives and will receive a just reward. Our salvation will always be secure in Christ, but what we do with our salvation still matters. We can rejoice and live in the security of knowing Jesus as our Savior, but we should never let our security as believers keep us from living in purity and good works.

✤ ✤ ✤

Hebrews Six

One of the toughest passages in the Bible to understand is Hebrews Chapter 6. This passage has been a source of confusion, fear, and misunderstanding for centuries. I know this passage is often used to teach that Christians can lose their salvation by "falling away," but we must be careful not to overlook the basic context of this passage in order to determine what the author of Hebrews was really writing about.

To examine this passage carefully, we must understand that the book of Hebrews in the Bible was originally a letter that was written to Jews who had believed in Jesus as the promised Messiah. They had been raised within the Jewish religion and had practiced the Jewish faith all of their lives. Now, as Christians, they were being taught Jesus was the final, complete, and ultimate sacrifice; therefore, they no longer had any need of participating in the Jewish sacrifices and religious ceremonies.

These Jewish believers were struggling with these life-altering changes, and some were falling back into their old religious practices. There was a great deal of pressure being placed upon them by family, friends, Jewish leaders, and even some other Christians who were teaching it was necessary to continue in the Law of Moses and to carry out the sacrifices of goats and bulls.

The writer of Hebrews was trying to show the Jewish Christians it was not necessary to sacrifice any more and that doing so was really disgracing the sacrifice Jesus made on their behalf. He was also warning them of the dangers of falling back into the Law. Falling into sin *was not* the issue at hand.

In Hebrews 5:11–6:3 the writer points out that these Christians should be beyond such elementary teachings.

> Concerning him we have much to say, and it is hard to explain, since you have become dull of hearing. For though by this time you ought to be teachers, you have need again for someone to teach you the elementary principals of the oracles of God, and you have come to need milk and not solid food. For everyone who partakes only of milk is not accustomed to the word of righteousness, for he is an infant. But solid food is for the mature, who because of practice have their senses trained to discern good and evil. Therefore leaving the elementary teaching about the Christ, let us press on to maturity, not laying again a foundation of repentance from dead works and of faith toward God, of instruction about washing and laying on of hands, and the resurrection of the dead and eternal judgment. And this we will do, if God permits.

There is no room for doubt that the author is writing to Christians. The Jewish believers should have been able to teach and move on to deeper biblical truths, but they had fallen back into old practices and were becoming more and more confused. This is what we see being described in Hebrews 6:4–6.

For in the case of those who have once been enlightened and have tasted of the heavenly gift and have been made partakers of the Holy Spirit, and have tasted the good word of God and the powers of the age to come, and then have fallen away, it is impossible to renew them again to repentance, since they again crucify to themselves the Son of God and put Him to open shame.

The Jewish Christians who had seen the light, been sealed with the Holy Spirit, and witnessed the workings of God, were going back to their Jewish religious practices and were again sacrificing animals as the Law prescribed, but we are repeatedly told in Hebrews that Jesus fulfilled the requirements of the Law once and for all. We find this in Hebrews 7:27, 9:12, and 10:10–14.

Who does not need daily, like those high priests, to offer up sacrifices, first for His own sins and then for the sins of the people, because He did once for all when He offered up Himself.

And not through the blood of goats and calves, but through His own blood, He entered the holy place once for all, having obtained eternal redemption.

By this will we have been sanctified through the offering of the body of Jesus once for all. Every priest stands daily ministering and offering time after time the same sacrifices, which can never take away sins; but He, having offered one sacrifice for sins for all time, SAT DOWN AT THE RIGHT HAND OF GOD, waiting from that time onward UNTIL HIS ENEMIES BE MADE A FOOTSTOOL FOR HIS FEET. For by one offering he has perfected for all time those who are sanctified.

The writer of Hebrews was trying to explain to the Jewish Christians that it was absolutely unnecessary to offer up any more sacrifices, since Jesus was the perfect and ultimate sacrifice—that one sacrifice was sufficient, and anyone who is cleansed of sin by that sacrifice is cleansed once and for all. Therefore, it is no longer necessary to offer a sacrifice.

To offer up sacrifices would be a "dead work," and it would put Jesus to open shame by declaring that His sacrifice was not sufficient. These were the very "dead works" that could not have saved them in the first place.

If the Christians felt they needed to carry out the religious ceremonies and sacrifices in order to be forgiven, then they were *falling away* from the freedom that Jesus died to give them. They would then be placing themselves back under the yoke of the Law.

However, to do so would not cause them to lose their salvation, since salvation is not based on good works or religious ceremony. The author did not proclaim that the Jewish Christians who fell away by mistakenly offering sacrifices would lose their salvation. However, he did write that they could not be brought back to repentance.

Repentance and salvation are not the same things! Repentance means to change your mind or to change course. Salvation is eternal life. We cannot be saved without first repenting, but there will also be times in which we will need to repent after we are saved, when we find ourselves in sin or error.

From what did these believers need to repent? Dead works! That is what Hebrews 6:1 clearly tells us. The Jewish Christians had fallen back into dead works. What dead works? Believing that following the Jewish sacrifices and ceremonies were necessary to maintain salvation. They had been deceived into believing that Jesus' dying on the cross for their sins was not enough to ensure their forgiveness once for all. As a result of this error, they began to depend again on carrying out the Jewish religious duties. They may also have simply succumbed to the pressure of family, friends, or neighbors who were not pleased with their having given up the Jewish customs. The demand to continue to live as a Jew must have been overwhelming.

Whatever the cause, these Christians began to fall back into the Law, just as the Christians in Galatia had done. Paul writes about this in Galatians 3:1–3.

> You foolish Galatians, who has bewitched you, before whose eyes Jesus Christ was publicly portrayed as crucified? This is the only thing I want to find out from you: did you receive the Spirit by the works of the Law, or by hearing with faith? Are you so foolish? Having begun by the Spirit, are you now being perfected by the flesh?

The Galatians had obviously received the Spirit, and this can only happen once a person has believed in Jesus as their Lord and Savior. Likewise, the Christians written about in Hebrews had become "partakers of the Holy Spirit."

The issue at hand was not salvation. No, instead, it was repenting from dead works. The Christians were wasting their time sacrificing animals and they were disgracing the name of Christ by doing so. Both of these were wrong and shameful, but that does not negate the fact that they were sealed by the Holy Spirit and had already been given eternal life. They were indeed Christians even though they had fallen into error.

Galatians 5:14 gives us another look into the matter.

> You who are trying to be justified by the law have been alienated from Christ; you have fallen away from grace. (NIV)

Please note that Paul was writing to people who were trying to be justified by the law, they were trying to earn or maintain salvation through adherence to Jewish customs. His warning had nothing to do with sinful living! The Galatians had been deceived and were living in bondage because of false teaching. That is what it means to have fallen from grace!

If falling into error could cause us to lose our salvation, then none of us would have any hope of attaining eternal life, for we all slip into error at times; none of us is perfect, nor do any of us completely know and follow all of God's truth perfectly. (Even Peter, James, and Barnabas were guilty of falling into error, and Paul had to confront them about the problem, according to Galatians 2:11–14.)

If we fail to repent when our error is exposed, we will have to bear the consequences such a choice brings. So, what would be the result of a life invested in dead works? We are told in Hebrews 6:7–8.

> For ground that drinks the rain which often falls on it and brings forth vegetation useful to those for whose sake it is also tilled, receives a blessing from God; but if it yields thorns and thistles, it is worthless and close to being cursed, and it ends up being burned.

Can you see the connection here? Dead works produce thorns and thistles, but godly and good works produce useful fruit. Which of these does God reward and which does He consume with fire? Doesn't this connect with the images we find in 1 Corinthians 3:10–15 and John 15:1–11 about bearing fruit and being tested by fire?

Furthermore, Hebrews 6:9–12 really highlights the main focus of this entire passage.

> But, beloved, we are convinced of better things concerning you, and things that accompany salvation, though we are speaking in this way. For God is not unjust so as to forget your work and the love which you have shown toward His name, in having ministered and in still ministering to the saints. And we desire that each one of you show the same diligence so as to realize the full assurance of hope until the end, so that you will not be sluggish, but imitators of those who through faith and patience inherit the promises.

The writer of Hebrews is clearly talking about works, and we know that we are not saved by works! He is talking about those things that *accompany salvation*, not that which gives us salvation. We have been given promises that extend beyond salvation. Those promises can be ours if we will do good works in the name of Jesus, and we are never saved by imitating people or through diligence. No, we are only saved by grace through faith.

Once Jesus has forgiven us because we have received Him as our Lord and Savior, we are eternally forgiven; all of our sins are forgiven and forgotten. A person does not move from a state of saved to unsaved, forgiven to unforgiven. This is not possible. A person has either trusted in Christ and therefore received forgiveness and eternal life, or they have not. If a person can become unforgiven, then the blood of Christ was insufficient, and there would be need for an additional sacrifice each time a person sinned.

We are saved by grace and have eternal security in Christ, but we will be judged according to our works. Good and godly works will be rewarded. Ungodly, selfish, or empty religious works will be consumed and will result in the loss of rewards. This is taught here in Hebrews 6 and throughout the entire New Testament.

�֎ ✖ ֎

Fearing God

For most of my early Christian walk, I was never taught to fear God. I cannot recollect having ever heard a sermon about fearing God as a Christian. Sure, I remember listening to many sermons that warned me to seek salvation and to fear hell, but I do not recall ever learning about the commandment for *Christians* to fear God.

Instead, I remember many passages about love. I have no problem with learning about God's love for us and our need to love Him, but looking back, it seems most of those messages had an incomplete view of love. They were lopsided and elementary in nature, ignoring the fact that God commands us to fear Him as our Father.

I know God loves me. I realize that He sent His only begotten Son to die for my sins (John 3:16). I also recognize that God is love (1 John 4:16). And, I understand that through God's love and grace, I have been adopted into His holy family (1 John 3:1). I have heard countless messages and Sunday school lessons about these truths, yet I do not remember ever hearing anyone tell me to fear God *because* He is my heavenly Father.

Then I read 1 Peter 1:17–19.

> If you address as Father the One who impartially judges according to each one's work, conduct yourselves in fear during your stay on earth; knowing that you were not redeemed with perishable things like silver or gold from

your futile way of life inherited from your forefathers, but with precious blood, as of a lamb unblemished and spotless, the blood of Christ.

There can be no doubt after reading this short passage that if we are Christians, then we should fear God. I know this may go completely against what you have been taught. Quite frankly, it nearly knocked me over the first time God opened my eyes to this truth.

But, as I have studied the Bible more thoroughly, I have begun to see why this is so important. I have also come to see this does not contradict or counteract God's love. Hebrews 12:7–8 give us more to think about.

> It is for discipline that you endure; God deals with you as with sons; for what son is there whom his father does not discipline? But if you are without discipline, of which all have become partakers, then you are illegitimate children and not sons.

Could this be any clearer? If we are children of God, then we should expect to be disciplined by our Father. If we are not disciplined, then we are not truly His children. God's love for His children compels Him to discipline us.

Should we fear this discipline? Of course! Hebrews 12:11 explains why.

> All discipline for the moment seems not to be joyful, but sorrowful; yet to those who have been trained by it, afterwards it yields the peaceful fruit of righteousness.

Discipline is painful! It hurts, and we do not enjoy it; otherwise, it wouldn't be true discipline. After all, what father punishes and disciplines his child by giving him candy, increasing his allowance, or buying him a new gadget? Discipline brings temporary sorrow, but it yields godly fruit.

As I mentioned in an earlier chapter, God, as our heavenly Father, will discipline us. When He does, it is a painful but necessary thing, for that is the only way we learn how to repent from dead works and begin to produce godly fruit in our lives. Discipline is intended to produce obedience, which, in turn, produces righteous behavior.

I truly see how it is possible to simultaneously fear and love God by looking at my relationship with my dad. He is a good man who loves me very much. When I was growing up, I used to love to spend time doing things with him, especially fishing. We would have a wonderful time together, and I looked up to him. I never worried about my father hurting me, abusing me, or doing anything that would harm me. I knew dad would protect me, provide for me, guide me, and always look out for my best interest. He proved this time and time again.

Yet, when I had been doing something I knew was wrong, I did not want to be around dad because I feared him. I knew if I broke his rules and acted rebellious, discipline was coming my way. The discipline was always temporary, but it was painful, and it definitely got my attention. Now, by looking at my earthly father, I can see how I can both love and fear my heavenly Father. (I know that some earthly fathers are poor models of God. Not everyone is blessed with a loving, caring, and strong dad, but almost everyone has a teacher, grandparent, coach, or someone else who might fit this example well.)

You might believe we are not supposed to fear God, based on 1 John 4:18.

> There is no fear in love; but perfect love casts out fear, because fear involves punishment, and the one who fears is not perfected in love.

It would be easy to read this passage and conclude that if we truly love God, then we should never fear Him. In fact, that is how I often hear or read this scripture being taught. The only problem is this belief completely contradicts the verses we just looked at in 1 Peter and Hebrews.

So, what is the correct way to interpret this passage? Look at the context. Read 1 John 4:15–17.

> Whoever confesses that Jesus is the Son of God, God abides in him, and he in God. We have come to know and have believed the love which God has for us. God is love, and the one who abides in love abides in God, and God abides in him. By this, love is perfected with us, so that we may have confidence in the day of judgment; because as He is, so also we are in this world.

The context seems to indicate John is talking about salvation. If we have confessed Jesus as the Son of God, then we are saved. If we are saved, God abides in us, and we in Him. This should bring us comfort, knowing that on the Day of Judgment we will be safe from condemnation.

We do not have to fear being condemned or cast out of salvation. In other words, we do not have to fear punishment, since we have been eternally forgiven.

As Christians, we can fear the discipline of God without having to fear the eternal punishment for our sins. We can rest in the security of Christ and not fear that God will condemn us if we make a mistake or fall into error. A person is only condemned if he or she does not believe in Jesus! (John 3:16–18, 36; 5:24)

Now, look into Psalm 103:8–14. Here we can see just how closely fearing God and loving God are connected.

> The Lord is compassionate and gracious, Slow to anger and abounding in lovingkindness. He will not always strive with us, nor will He keep His anger forever. He has not dealt with us according to our sins, nor rewarded us according to our iniquities. For as high as the heavens are above the earth, so great is His lovingkindness toward those who fear Him. As far as the east is from the west, so far has He removed our transgressions from us. Just as a father has compassion on his children, so the Lord has compassion on those who fear Him. For He Himself knows our frame; He is mindful that we are but dust.

In God's great love and mercy, He sent Jesus to take our place and to remove our sins. God is gracious and compassionate, and He has made a way for us to be forgiven and to have eternal life. God has placed the full punishment for sin upon Jesus, once and for all. And, for those who are in Christ Jesus, there is no more condemnation (Romans 8:1).

But, I hope you can see this does not mean God will ignore sinful living. He will not punish us, since Jesus has already taken the punishment in our place, but God will discipline us in order to teach us a new and better way of living.

I know this may be confusing since we often consider punishment and discipline as interchangeable words. However, punishment is the payment of a penalty for doing something wrong and discipline is the teaching and reinforcement of acceptable behavior. Punishment is a consequence and penalty of bad behavior while discipline aims to train a person to avoid bad behavior or to teach them better behavior. Can you see the difference?

Christians, take heed. We are not beyond the discipline of our Father in heaven. If we continue to willfully sin and reject the conviction of the Holy Spirit, we can expect to be disciplined. He will not take away our salvation, since we are secure in Christ, but God will get our attention and teach us a lesson, and those lessons are often painful.

We should not consider God's lovingkindness as an indicator that God does not hold His children accountable. That would be a grave mistake, one that could lead to careless and fruitless living. Instead, we should never forget that being held accountable is an indicator of true love.

To know God is to fear God. To fear God is to love God. To love God is to obey His commands and to produce fruit for His kingdom. We need to take the warnings of the Bible very seriously. We should never assume we are beyond God's discipline or correction.

❊ ❊ ❊

The Promises

Balance is so important in our relationship with God. We do need to fear God and understand His justice and power, but we also need to know God is generous and kind. If we only focus on the fear of God, we will most likely run from Him and fail to grow in relationship with our heavenly Father. To prevent this from happening, we need to know God is good, kind, longsuffering, and giving.

Recently, I was deeply touched by Malachi 3:13–15. It opened my eyes to a great truth.

> "Your words have been arrogant against Me," says the Lord. "Yet you say, 'What have we spoken against You?' You have said, 'It is vain to serve God; and what profit is it that we have kept His charge, and that we have walked in mourning before the Lord of hosts? So now we call the arrogant blessed; not only are the doers of wickedness built up but they also test God and escape.'"

This passage helped me to see that what we think about God matters greatly because it drives our actions and attitudes in life.

If we see God as a taker and an overbearing tyrant, then we will not seek Him or give our hearts to Him. However, if we view God as a giver who has made incredible promises to those who follow Him, we are more likely to give Him our loyalty.

The Israelites were going through the motions, but they were not really seeking the promises of God. This passage reveals they did not truly believe it was worth it to seek after and obey the Lord. This caused them to serve only half-heartedly and to look upon wicked people as those who were blessed. This attitude led them into idolatry and sinful activities. They did not believe God would bless them and reward them for obedience; therefore, their hearts led them astray. In other words, they began to pursue the things they believed would bring them the most joy and happiness in life.

This passage reaffirmed a truth for me: our behavior follows our beliefs. That is probably why Romans 12:2 directly connects our minds with our behavior.

> And do not be conformed to this world, but be transformed by the renewing of your mind, so that you may prove what the will of God is, that which is good and acceptable and perfect.

I hope you can see just how important this connection is; it is truly life changing. Our actions will follow our beliefs, and if we do not believe it is worth it to seek and obey God, then we will not do so, no matter how much we know we should. Do you see the reality in this? Do you see the danger?

It has to be worth it to serve God in our own minds. If we do not believe it is truly profitable for us to serve God, then we will never love Him with all of our heart, soul, and mind. And, no matter how hard we try, we will never be able to break out of our old ways and embrace His ways.

That was the reality I found myself in a few years ago. I was trying to obey God based only on fear, and I thought it was sinful to seek the blessings and favor of God. Once I began to understand how much He has promised us and how much He wants to bless us, I began to serve Him in a whole new way.

God has made us many promises. The promises are real and are intended to motivate us. Hebrews 11:6 is a perfect example of this.

> And without faith it is impossible to please Him, for he who comes to God must believe that He is and that He is a rewarder of those who seek Him.

Life changing faith is not simply believing a god exists or that God is real. True, life-altering faith happens only when we believe God is a "rewarder of those who seek Him."

The Lord wants us to see that He is faithful, good, and generous. I believe that is why the Bible is full of assurances that should draw us closer to our loving, heavenly Father. For example, Matthew 6:33 gives us an incredible promise.

> But seek first His kingdom and His righteousness, and all these things will be added to you.

Romans 8:28 contains an incredible promise as well.

> And we know that God causes all things to work together for good to those who love God, to those who are called according to His purpose.

And James 1:12 give us another promise.

> Blessed is a man who preservers under trial; for once he has been approved, he will receive the crown of life which the Lord has promised to those who love Him.

So, if you want to learn to seek God with all of your heart, soul, and mind, you need to get to know the promises of God and believe they are real. You also need to realize that God wants to bless *you* personally! This is extremely important; you have to believe that God's promises are literally available to you if they are going to have any real influence in your life.

By placing our faith in the goodness, faithfulness, and love of God, we can sink our teeth into these promises so they will inspire us and guide us daily. The more we believe God is both willing and able to fulfill these pledges, the greater the odds are we will obey Him and make wise, godly choices.

I want to encourage you to make a list of God's promises that touch you and inspire you. Let those scriptures become a source of hope, comfort, wisdom, and strength. As you put your trust in these promises of God, you will find it easier to follow Him and to love others as yourself.

We need to know it is worth it to seek God. We need to know His promises are real and that He is faithful. As we place our trust in His promises, our lives will change, and we will reap the rewards of godliness.

※ ※ ※

Using the Broken

God calls those who are messed up, fouled up, and broken. This is an amazing fact that permeates all of scripture. I cannot find anyone in the Bible (other than Jesus) who was perfect, but I can see many who were defeated, damaged, and weak who became useful in God's hands. I also know many Christians today who would fall into that same category.

God is not waiting for you to act perfectly or to walk without sin before He is willing to use you; what He is looking for is a responsive heart. God does not call and use perfect people; otherwise, He would never be able to use any of us. However, He calls and uses those who are broken but willing to repent and seek Him.

The list of people God used who had failures and foul ups is incredible. We can name Moses, who was a murderer, or Jacob, who was a liar and a thief. There is also David, who wound up committing adultery and then murdering to cover up his sinful behavior. Peter is the poster child for making mistakes, and Paul was guilty of persecuting Christians prior to his conversion. God called and used harlots, thieves, murderers, and others who couldn't measure up.

The key to their usefulness was not their perfect reputations or their ability to never make a sinful choice; instead, their usefulness was mainly determined by their willingness to repent.

Psalm 51:1-4 reveals King David's heart. It helps us to see how deeply he regretted his sinful choices and how he confessed his sinfulness and asked for God's grace.

> Be gracious to me, O God, according to Your lovingkindness; according to the greatness of Your compassion blot out my transgressions. Wash me thoroughly from my iniquity and cleanse me from my sin. For I know my transgressions, and my sin is ever before me. Against You, You only, I have sinned and done what is evil in Your sight, so that You are justified when You speak and blameless when You judge.

Verses 10-13 give us even more insight into the depths of David's repentance.

> Create in me a clean heart, O God, and renew a steadfast spirit within me. Do not cast me away from Your presence and do not take Your Holy Spirit from me. Restore to me the joy of Your salvation and sustain me with a willing spirit. Then I will teach transgressors Your ways, and sinners will be converted to You.

David acknowledged his sins and admitted he had offended God and sinned against Him. David also knew he could not make up for his mistakes but could only ask for God's mercy and grace. With this kind of "broken and contrite heart," David was useful in the Master's hands.

Peter is another example given to us. We know Peter made many mistakes, but the one that sticks out the most

Using the Broken

is his denial of knowing Jesus. We are given the account of Peter's shameful act in Mark 14:66–72.

> While Peter was below in the courtyard, one of the servant girls of the high priest came by. When she saw Peter warming himself, she looked closely at him, "You also were with that Nazarene. Jesus," she said. But he denied it. "I don't know or understand what you're talking about," he said, and went out into the entryway. When the servant girl saw him there, she said again to those standing around, "This fellow is one of them." Again he denied it. After a little while, those standing near said to Peter, "Surely you are one of them, for you are Galilean." He began to call down curses on himself, and he swore to them, "I don't know this man you're talking about." Immediately the rooster crowed the second time. Then Peter remembered the word Jesus had spoken to him: "Before the rooster crows twice you will disown me three times." And he broke down and wept. (NIV)

We know Peter messed up. He was afraid and denied Jesus, just as the Lord had said he would. Peter, the man who had sworn he would die for Jesus' sake, lied about knowing the One whom he had called the Christ. There is no doubt Peter blew it.

But, we can also see that Peter repented. Once he realized what he had done, his heart was broken. He wept with remorse, knowing he had denied Jesus before men.

Yet, even though he had failed miserably, Jesus was not through with Peter. Peter learned from his mistake. He changed course and later went about risking his life in order to proclaim the name of Jesus openly and boldly. In fact, Peter was imprisoned, abused, tortured, and eventually killed because he refused to deny Jesus again.

Peter was by no means perfect, but he did have a repentant heart. When confronted with his sin, he was willing to change his mind and actions. Because of this, he was extremely useful to the Master.

You, too, may have made bad choices and sinful mistakes in your life. That does not disqualify you from being useful in the kingdom of God. If you are willing to admit your failures, ask for God's grace, and change your actions, then you will be a vessel of honor, useful to the Master for all good works.

Furthermore, you may currently be rebelling against God or caught up in a sinful habit. If that is the case, you need to repent and offer yourself to the service of your Master, just as King David and Peter did. If you do not, the consequences can be terrible. Plus, you will miss out on the joy and fulfillment of serving God and others, if you continue down the wrong path. Please consider both the promises and warnings of the Bible. Let them guide and empower you.

✤ ✤ ✤

Fruit in Keeping with Repentance

If God is convicting you through the passages I've referenced and the words I have written, then please don't hesitate to repent and seek Him for forgiveness, healing, and instruction. If you are a child of God, He wants to use you. If you are not willing to repent, you stand the risk of being "cut off." He is a holy God who is full of loving kindness and mercy, but don't think He will hold back His discipline from those whom He loves. After all, we are told time and again of God's love for Israel, yet they often felt the sting of God's "tough love."

John the Baptist came preaching repentance. Mark 1:4 and Acts 13:23–24 verify this remark.

> John the Baptist appeared in the wilderness preaching a baptism of repentance for the forgiveness of sins.

> From the descendants of this man, according to promise, God has brought to Israel as Savior, Jesus, after John had proclaimed before his coming a baptism of repentance to all the people of Israel.

John was not alone in his call to repentance. Jesus Himself preached mankind needed to repent. Matthew 4:17 is just one verse that confirms this.

> From that time Jesus began to preach and say, "Repent, for the kingdom of heaven is at hand."

This message of repentance continued after Jesus ascended into heaven. Peter and the other disciples called not only Israel to repent but the gentiles as well. Acts 2:38 may have been the first time Peter preached repentance, but it certainly wasn't his last.

> Peter said to them, "Repent, and each of you be baptized in the name of Jesus Christ for the forgiveness of your sins; and you will receive the gift of the Holy Spirit."

Repentance must occur if we hope to have a close relationship with the Lord. It is essential to salvation, and it is essential to our spiritual growth and ability to bear fruit.

Paul understood this, and that is why he was so tough on those whom he loved. Paul wrote strong letters to fellow Christians because he knew they were falling away from obedience and good works. 2 Corinthians 7:8–9 displays Paul's emotions and explains why he was so bold.

> For though I caused you sorrow by my letter, I do not regret it; though I did regret it—for I see that that letter caused you sorrow, though only for a while—I now rejoice, not that you were made sorrowful, but that you were made sorrowful to the point of repentance; for you were made sorrowful according to the will of God, so that you might not suffer loss in anything through us.

Do you see here the plea of Paul's heart? He did not want to make his fellow Christians sorrowful, but he knew he had to tell them the truth, and his sorrow turned to joy once he saw they were willing to repent.

Also, notice Paul mentioned he did not want them to suffer loss. Paul was connecting their willingness to repent with the rewards that they were going to receive. Their willingness to repent would clear the way for good works, which would then result in fruitful living, and, therefore, they would receive glorious rewards.

Christians, there are times when we need to repent! There are times when we are confronted by the truth and are exposed as disobedient children of God. If we do not repent, we will indeed face the consequences.

I believe God is calling out to His children, calling us to repent and return to purity and good works. I hear the call of John the Baptist in Matthew 3:7–9 as he confronted the Pharisees and Sadducees.

> But when he saw many of the Pharisees and Sadducees coming for baptism, he said to them, "You brood of vipers, who warned you to flee from the wrath to come? Therefore bear fruit in keeping with repentance; and do not suppose that you can say to yourselves, 'We have Abraham for our father'; for I say to you that from these stones God is able to raise up children to Abraham."

Jesus also shows us in Revelation 2:4–5 how important it is for Christians to repent when they have stumbled.

> But I have this against you, that you have left your first love. Therefore remember from where you have fallen, and repent and do the deeds you did at first; for else I am coming to you and will remove your lampstand out of its place—unless you repent.

Likewise, we can read of Paul's cry for Christians to bear fruit in keeping with repentance. Acts 26:19–20 give us just a glimpse of Paul's zeal.

> So, King Agrippa, I did not prove disobedient to the heavenly vision, but kept declaring both to those of Damascus first, and also at Jerusalem and then throughout all the region of Judea, and even to the Gentiles, that they should repent and turn to God, performing deeds appropriate to repentance.

Finally, Luke 22:31–32 gives us the best picture of the connection between repentance and service to God.

> Simon, Simon, behold, Satan has demanded permission to sift you like wheat; but I have prayed for you, that your faith may not fail; and you, when once you have turned again, strengthen your brothers.

We see here the warning and encouragement that Jesus gave Simon Peter only hours before he would deny the Lord three times. Jesus knew Peter would fail due to fear and confusion. He knew Satan would attack him and drive him to the point of disowning his Lord.

Yet, Jesus interceded for Peter and prayed that, though he would stumble, he would not continue to deny Him. Jesus knew Peter would repent. Jesus knew his disciple would confess his sin and once again seek to declare him as the Christ.

But notice, Jesus tells Peter his calling to strengthen his fellow Christians would come *after* he repented. Jesus knew Peter would sincerely regret his mistake and ask for forgiveness. Once he did, he would be able to go about bearing fruit as the leader of the early church. In fact, this painful event may have been a major catalyst in Peter's zeal for sharing Christ with others.

Can you see the connection to your own calling? Scripture clearly shows Paul, John the Baptist, and even Jesus Himself preached that those who wanted to be saved must repent. But they also taught that Christians who wanted to bear godly fruit must repent when they fall into disobedience, if they hoped to bear fruit for the kingdom of God.

❈ ❈ ❈

Tombs and Dishes

Jesus was not always soft-spoken despite our modern depictions of Him. His foremost concern was not making people feel good about themselves. In fact, Jesus was often very bold and direct, even when that meant His words were offensive to some people. This bothered his disciples. They seemed to have wanted Jesus to be a little more politically correct. Just imagine the scene that unfolded in Matthew 15:10–14.

> After Jesus called the crowd to Him, He said to them, "Hear and understand. It is not what enters into the mouth that defiles the man, but what proceeds out of the mouth, this defiles the man." Then the disciples came and said to Him, "Do You know that the Pharisees were offended when they heard the statement?" But He answered and said, "Every plant which My heavenly Father did not plant shall be uprooted. Let them alone; they are blind guides of the blind. And if a blind man guides a blind man, both will fall into a pit."

The simple truth is God loves us enough to be bold with us. He loves us enough to hurt our feelings when it is for our good. The Lord is not concerned with offending us. What He cares about is our holiness and willingness to bear godly fruit in His name.

Please do not ignore or reason away this truth. Our heavenly Father sincerely wants us to be righteous and zealous for good works. He doesn't want us to put on a show. That is not good enough. No, God wants His children to be pure inside and out. This is exemplified in Matthew 23:23-24.

> Woe to you, scribes and Pharisees, hypocrites! For you tithe mint and dill and cumin, and have neglected the weightier provisions of the law: justice and mercy and faithfulness; but these are the things you should have done without neglecting the others.

Jesus boldly confronted the hypocrisy of the religious leaders of His time. They put on a show and carried out their religious duties, but they were careless with their personal purity and faithful service to others. They wanted everyone to think they were holy, but they were not, not as God defines it.

He went on in His harsh assessment of their hypocrisy in Matthew 23:25-28.

> Woe to you, scribes and Pharisees, hypocrites! For you clean the outside of the cup and of the dish, but inside they are full of robbery and self-indulgence. You blind Pharisee, first clean the inside of the cup and of the dish, so that the outside may become clean also. Woe to you, scribes and Pharisees, hypocrites! For you are like whitewashed tombs which on the outside appear beautiful, but inside they are full of dead men's bones and all uncleanness. So you, too, outwardly appear righteous to men, but inwardly you are full of hypocrisy and lawlessness.

Jesus hates hypocrisy. The Pharisees were masters of disguise; they would act holy, devout, and caring in public, but behind closed doors, they were devils. These religious leaders would steal and kill if it made them money or gave them power. They were immoral and gave into lust as if it didn't matter at all. Their actions in private revealed the defilement within.

Jesus exposed them. He confronted their hypocrisy and never bought into their holy act. The same can be said of us today. Jesus will expose and confront us. The word of God and the Holy Spirit will convict us and get our attention when we are living in opposition to God's plans and purposes. A godly appearance and a holy charade will not cover our sins.

If you truly want to be a vessel of honor, then your inner self is going to have to be clean. God knows our hearts and sees our every step. He knows if we are just acting religious and putting on a show. He can look deep into our hearts and detect if we are harboring secret sins and ungodliness within.

God calls us to *true* holiness and love. God hates insincerity and pretense and will confront us boldly when we live like the Scribes and Pharisees. Because He loves us so deeply, Jesus would rather hurt our feelings or offend us than leave us alone in our sinful behavior.

Reading the Bible, church attendance, teaching a Sunday school class, tithing, or any other religious activity should never be considered as a way to make up for sinful activity. If you are looking at pornography or stealing from your company throughout the week but feel that going to church every time the doors are open balances it out, you are sadly mistaken. This kind of reasoning didn't work for the Pharisees, and it will not work for us today.

If we hope to be useful to the Master for all good works, then we must strive to live a life of purity and love from the inside out. Nothing else will do.

❖ ❖ ❖

Integrity

God is calling His children to be men and women of integrity. This is nothing new; God has been issuing the same decree since the beginning of time.

When Adam and Eve were in the garden, God gave them everything to enjoy, jobs to do, and a simple command to obey His instructions. God did not place a burdensome amount of restrictions upon Adam and Eve; in fact, we can only read of a few specific instructions.

Genesis 2:27–28 gives us the first instructions ever given to mankind: be fruitful, increase in number, and rule over creation.

> God created man in His own image, in the image of God He created him: male and female He created them. God blessed them; and God said to them, "Be fruitful and multiply, and fill the earth, and subdue it; and rule over the fish of the sea and the birds of the sky and over every living thing that move on the earth."

The next instructions are found in Genesis 2:15: Work in the Garden of Eden.

> Then the Lord God took the man and put him into the garden of Eden to cultivate it and keep it.

The third instruction is located in Genesis 2:16–17: Do not eat from the tree of the knowledge of good and evil.

> The Lord God commanded the man, saying, "From any tree in the garden you may eat freely; but from the tree of the knowledge of good and evil you shall not eat, for in the day that you eat from it you will surely die."

I find it interesting that we can see within these simple commands two major things: bear fruit and obey.

We can also see how obeying impacts fruit bearing. When Adam and Eve sinned, they were "cut off," or "taken away," from the garden. This directly impacted their ability to fulfill their calling to work the garden and bear fruit. As a result of their sin, they had to live under a curse. That curse made it more difficult to enjoy the life God had given them. As a direct result of their sin, bearing children and fruit was going to be painful, according to Genesis 3:16–19.

> To the woman He said, "I will greatly multiply your pain in childbirth, in pain you will bring forth children; yet your desire will be for your husband, and he will rule over you." Then to Adam He said, "Because you have listened to the voice of your wife, and have eaten from the tree about which I commanded you, saying, 'You shall not eat from it'; cursed is the ground because of you; in toil you will eat of it all the days of your life. Both thorns and thistles it shall grow for you; and you will eat the plants of the field; by the sweat of your face you will eat bread, till you return to the ground, because from it you were taken; for you are dust, and to dust you shall return."

The consequences of Adam and Eve's sins were real and life changing. They were no longer able to enjoy all God had offered them, and they faced hardship in trying to produce children and food. Sin interfered with God's intended plans and purposes, and it made Adam and Eve's lives more difficult.

As we have already seen, this theme continues to thread all the way through scripture, and the consequence of their sin is still felt today.

If Adam and Eve hoped to produce the fruitful work God created them for, then they were going to have to remain faithful and obedient. In other words, they were going to have to remain committed to integrity.

God created mankind to work and to bear fruit. He then gave us some guidelines by which we should live so we will be able to fulfill this calling. It requires continued obedience to be the people God wants us to be. In other words, we must consistently be honest, trustworthy, upright, and honorable if we hope to reach our full potential as children of God.

People with integrity are the same day in and day out. They do not allow circumstance to determine their values, and they live by the same guiding principals both in public and in private.

Throughout history, God has instructed His followers to live lives of integrity. This same ideal can be seen as we read 1 Kings 9:1–5.

> Now it came about when Solomon had finished building the house of the Lord, and the king's house, and all that Solomon desired to do, that the Lord appeared to Solomon a second time, as he had appeared to Him at Gibeon. The Lord said to him, "I have heard your prayer and your

supplication, which you have made before Me; I have consecrated this house which you have built by putting My name there forever, and My eyes and My heart will be there perpetually. As for you, if you will walk before Me as your father David walked, in integrity of heart and uprightness, doing according to all that I have commanded you and will keep My statues and My ordinances, then I will establish the throne of your kingdom over Israel forever, just as I promised to your father David, saying, 'You shall not lack a man on the throne of Israel.'"

As you can see, God directed Solomon to live a life of integrity. He then told the king that if he would live in obedience (continued integrity), then God would fulfill all that was promised. This would include the power, authority, and honor to continue to do fruitful works, for the throne came with the power, authority, and honor to accomplish great things in the name of God.

However, if Solomon failed to live a life of integrity, God would remove His hand of favor. The promise to establish Solomon's kingdom was conditional, and it all depended on Solomon's willingness to submit his life to God.

Jesus is our best example in this teaching. He alone was able to live a perfect life of integrity. He completely and totally obeyed God's will, and was therefore useful to the Father at all times. We know He was tempted to break God's commands, just as we are, yet He remained faithful, according to Hebrews 4:14–15.

> Therefore, since we have a great high priest who has passed through the heavens, Jesus the Son of God, let

us hold fast our confession. For we do not have a high priest who cannot sympathize with our weaknesses, but One who has been tempted in all things as we are, yet without sin.

Philippians 2:8 builds upon this truth.

Being found in appearance as a man, He humbled Himself by becoming obedient to the point of death, even death on a cross.

Obedience and complete integrity were essential in Christ's ministry to mankind. Had He given into temptation and pursued His own interest and desires, God would not have been able to use Him for the greatest fruit bearing calling of all time: the redemption of mankind.

Integrity is so important in the life of a Christian. Without it, we cannot fulfill our calling to be fruitful. Christ showed us the way, and He has promised to help us be both obedient and fruitful. To do that, He is working within us by the power and guidance of the word and the Holy Spirit. Now, we, as Children of God, must commit our lives to purity and good works if we hope to have the fullness of life that Jesus died to give us.

If we stumble, there is forgiveness. If we will repent and seek Him, He will restore us and use us for good things. However, if we refuse to repent, we face the possibility of being "cut off." This is a real and deliberate warning from God. He wants each of His children to bear fruit so as to bring glory to His name. Living in integrity is vital for this purpose.

�֍ �֍ ✯

Purposeful Living

We will not be men and women of integrity, vessels of honor, without setting our sights on holiness and purity. We must determine in our hearts that we are going to seek obedience to God above anything else in our lives.

Proverbs 29:18 gives us a scriptural look at the need for purposeful living.

> Where there is no vision, the people are unrestrained, but happy is he who keeps the law.

We must set godly goals if we hope to accomplish anything of meaning in life. We need to work toward a particular target. If we wander through life aimlessly, we will probably never achieve any success.

This is not only true in business, relationships, and sports, but it is also true in our spiritual growth. If we have no aspirations for spiritual maturity, then we will probably never develop past Christian infancy.

Every believer needs to have a vision for his life. Without vision, we are sure to wander about, never dealing with sin, and as a result, we will bear little or no fruit, always wavering and struggling with temptation and spiritual growth.

God tells us to seek Him and His kingdom repeatedly throughout the Bible. In other words, we must set our eyes upon a mark and then strive to reach that goal. God wants His children to set their sights on those things that please Him.

If integrity, purity, and obedience to all of God's word are not our aim, then we are sure to never reach these important heights. If you couldn't care less as to whether or not you are a vessel of honor, then I promise you will not be one.

God certainly wants us to take our spiritual maturity seriously. He also commands us to consider our fight against sin as something of utmost importance. Just read Matthew 18:8–9.

> If your hand or your foot causes you to stumble, cut it off and throw it from you; it is better for you to enter life crippled or lame, than to have two hands or two feet and be cast into the eternal fire. If your eye causes you to stumble, pluck it out and throw it from you. It is better for you to enter life with one eye, than to have two eyes and be cast into the fiery hell.

These are the very words of Jesus. Is there any doubt about the call to live in purity when we read these words? Are you this serious about your walk with God?

The Lord is not asking us to literally maim ourselves, but He is using exaggeration to teach us to take sin very seriously. He wants us to make personal purity and integrity main goals In our lives. It should be of utmost importance to those who call upon the name of the Lord.

We can see another example of the importance of setting our sights on purity. First Peter 1:13–16 give us a direct command to do so.

> Therefore, prepare your minds for action, keep sober in spirit, fix your hope completely on the grace to be brought

to you at the revelation of Jesus Christ. As obedient children, do not be conformed to the former lust which were yours in your ignorance, but like the Holy One who called you, be holy yourselves also in all your behavior; because it is written, "YOU SHALL BE HOLY, FOR I AM HOLY."

After reading this, can there be any doubt as to what God wants us to do? Can there be any excuse for allowing sin to continue unchecked in our lives?

We are saved by grace for sure. Notice that we are to *fix* our hope on grace alone. That is faith in Jesus. But as children of God, we are to obey Him by living in purity. We are supposed to work with Him as He conforms our lives to His holiness.

We must "fix" our eyes on this goal. We must strive to be pure and obedient children at all times. All of our behavior in all situations should reflect the holy God whom we call Father.

1 Peter 1:17–19 tells us just how serious this call to purity is in God's eyes.

> If you address as Father the One who impartially judges according to each one's works, conduct yourselves in fear during the time of your stay on earth; knowing that you were not redeemed with perishable things like silver or gold from your futile way of life inherited from your forefathers, but with precious blood, as of a lamb unblemished and spotless, the blood of Christ.

Can you see how serious God is about our willingness to commit ourselves to obedient and pure living? We do not become children of God by doing good works; we are adopted into His family by grace, through faith in Jesus (Ephesians 2:8-10).

Once we are redeemed by placing our faith in Christ, we become accountable to God as his children. With our salvation comes the responsibility to honor God in all we say and do, not for salvation, but because of our salvation.

As 1 Peter 1:17–19 so clearly states, God will judge us according to our works. This should build a healthy fear within us, a fear that causes us to strive for holiness and good works in our lives.

Is this possible? Can we live in purity and obedience? Yes! Psalm 119:9–11 gives us hope and instruction.

> How can a young man keep his way pure? By keeping it according to Your word. With all my heart I have sought You; Do not let me wander from Your commandments. Your word I have treasured in my heart, that I may not sin against You.

We will not live in complete perfection, but we can strive for holiness and love. By treasuring God's word and allowing it to transform us from within, we can be the people we were created to be.

If purity is your desire, you are sure to make wise choices. If obedience is your goal, you will learn to listen to His voice. If you treasure, truly treasure, God's word in your heart, you will make holy and God-honoring choices.

I hope you will take this chapter very seriously and spend some time thinking about who you really want to be and who God created you to be. Write your spiritual and practical goals down or tell someone what you would like to see change in your life. Pray and ask God to help you see who you can be in Christ. Don't settle for bondage and hopelessness. Set your sights on becoming a vessel of honor.

❖ ❖ ❖

The Time Is Now

We must get serious about our walk with God. Peter, Paul, John, and James all wrote with passion and zeal. They were completely committed to Jesus and His kingdom, so much so, that they were willing to die rather than deny Christ by what they said or did. These godly men also wrote to encourage others to give their lives totally to God. I must go back to Titus 2:11–14 to highlight Paul's own words.

> For the grace of God has appeared bringing salvation to all men, instructing us to deny ungodliness and worldly desires and to live sensibly, righteously and godly in the present age, looking for the blessed hope and the appearing of the glory of our great God and Savior, Jesus Christ, who gave Himself for us to redeem us from every lawless deed, and to purify for Himself a people for His possession, zealous for good deeds.

Paul compels us to be passionate followers of Christ. We are saved by grace through faith in Jesus, but we need to see how important pure living and good deeds are in God's eyes.

Jesus saved us by grace for a reason. He is building a kingdom! He redeemed us to be a people of purity and service. Paul knew this, lived it, and taught it.

How zealous are you in these two areas? How important is your personal holiness? Are you passionate about living in purity and obedience every moment of every day? How fervent are you about meeting the needs of others?

Jesus didn't call us to be lukewarm and mediocre. We know He is clear about the call to steadfast and zealous living. In His own words, Jesus sets the standard in Matthew 16:24–27.

> Then Jesus said to His disciples, "If anyone wishes to come after Me, he must deny himself, and take up his cross and follow Me. For whoever wishes to save his life will lose it; but whoever loses his life for My sake will find it. For what will it profit a man if he gains the whole world and forfeits his soul? Or what will a man give in exchange for his soul? For the Son of Man is going to come in the glory of His Father with His angels, and WILL THEN REPAY EVERY MAN ACCORDING TO HIS DEEDS."

If we are going to be devoted and passionate followers of Christ, it will not come without denying our fleshly desires. Jesus tells us to let go of our worldly and ungodly passions, and in their place become zealous for godliness and good works.

Paul gives us this same basic truth in Philippians 2:1–4 and Titus 3:8.

> Therefore if there is any encouragement in Christ, if there is any consolation of love, if there is any fellowship of the Spirit, if any affection and compassion, make my joy complete by being of the same mind, maintaining the same love, united in spirit, intent on one purpose. Do

> nothing from selfish or empty conceit, but with humility of mind regard one another as more important than yourselves; do not merely look out for your own personal interest, but also for the interest of others.
>
> This is a trust worthy statement; and concerning these things I want you to speak confidently, so that those who have believed God will be careful to engage in good deeds. These things are good and profitable for men.

Can there be any misunderstanding here? Paul clearly wanted the followers of Jesus to purposefully engage in doing good deeds. He saw this as an essential part of a Christian's life.

Personal purity and meeting the needs of others does not happen apart from choosing to deny sinful passions and to purposefully give ourselves to God. Our human nature is constantly tempted, and our ego constantly tries to convince us to please our own desires and needs. Galatians 5:13–24 exposes the battle that every Christian faces.

> You, my brothers, were called to be free. But do not use your freedom to indulge the sinful nature; rather serve one another in love. The entire law is summed up in a single command: "Love your neighbor as yourself." If you keep on biting and devouring each other, watch out or you will be destroyed by each other. So I say, live by the Spirit, and you will not gratify the desires of the sinful nature. For the sinful nature desires what is contrary to the Spirit, and the Spirit what is contrary to the sinful nature. They are in conflict with each other, so that you

do not do what you want. But if you are led by the Spirit, you are not under the law. The acts of the sinful nature are obvious: sexual immorality, impurity and debauchery; idolatry and witchcraft; hared, discord, jealousy, fits of rage, selfish ambition, dissensions, factions, and envy; drunkenness, orgies, and the like. I warn you, as I did before, that those who live like this will not inherit the kingdom of God. But the fruit of the Spirit is love, joy, peace, patience, kindness, goodness, faithfulness, gentleness and self-control. Against such things there is no law. Thos who belong to Christ Jesus have crucified the sinful nature with its passions and desires. (NIV)

Everyone who believes in Jesus as their Lord and Savior will face a real battle. The Holy Spirit will constantly try to draw them closer to God and urge them to help others in various ways. The nudging of the Spirit is gentle but consistent. At the same time, the flesh (the temptation of their own desires and passions) will contradict and fight against the Spirit's guidance; this is just simply part of being a believer.

Every time a Christian chooses to ignore the flesh in order to obey God, he or she "crucifies the flesh." Doing so honors God, produces fruit, and sows seeds of righteousness and rewards.

This is a real battle. It is one every Christian faces, but we are not hopeless. God has promised to help us endure and choose wisely. He has equipped us with His word and empowered us with the Holy Spirit. We can win the fight!

But, we must fight. Too often we ignore the call to battle and simply go about our daily lives, confused, empty and unfruitful, as we ignore the Spirit within us. That is not what God desires for us or from us.

God truly wants us to live abundant lives. He has promised to help us overcome and to be with us each step of the way. We can count on God's faithfulness and let His promises become the bedrock of our faith, but we must do our part as well. He has asked us to flee from sin and pursue righteousness.

Today is the day to fight! Today is the day to march out against sinful choices and attitudes. Every war begins with the first shot . . . today is the day to begin your spiritual war against the flesh.

In my own life I have seen how dangerous and painful delay can be. This has become apparent recently as we prepare to send our first child off to college. For eighteen years I've delayed and neglected my responsibility to save for her college education. I knew it was coming and I knew it would be expensive, but I never took the time to really plan for this moment. Now, we are faced with the possibility of having to go into debt in order to cover her tuition and fees, when we could have had the money saved up and set aside long ago, had we made better choices.

The issue was not a lack of information; we knew this day was coming and that it would require a lot of money. Likewise, the problem has not been a lack of income; we have never made a lot, but we have had enough to make ends meet. What it all boils down to is the fact that I just kept putting off until tomorrow what I should have being doing today! As a result, we are not well prepared. All of the worry, confusion, stress, and the possible debt could have been avoided had I done what I knew I needed to do along the way.

The old adage is true: the choices we make today determine our tomorrows. Please don't hesitate to do what you know is needed. If you do, you will look back one day and wonder why you didn't make changes earlier in your life. The time to make a difference is now!

�֍ ✧ ✧

We Have an Enemy

God loves us and desires good for our lives. He sent His Son to redeem us by taking our place on the cross as a holy and worthy sacrifice for our sins. God has boldly proclaimed His love, displayed His power, given us the opportunity to be saved by grace, and offered to empower us with His word and His Spirit.

But we also have an adversary. Satan wants to destroy us. He is our sworn enemy, and he is seeking to steal, kill, and destroy, according to John 10:10.

> The thief comes only to steal and to kill and to destroy; I have come that they may have life, and have it abundantly.

Can you see the contrast? God wants to give us a full and amazing life. Satan wants to rob us of our joy and fruitfulness. God is at work in and around us, calling us into the life He wants to give us. The enemy is doing all that is within his power to prevent us from experiencing and fulfilling God's plan and purpose. He schemes and plots and deceives in an effort to rob and destroy all that God offers us.

This truth is echoed throughout the Bible. 1 Peter 5:6–8 gives us another look into the heart of evil.

> Therefore humble yourselves under the mighty hand of God, that He may exalt you at the proper time, casting

> all your anxiety on Him, because He cares for you. Be of sober spirit, be on the alert. Your adversary, the devil, prowls around like a roaring lion, seeking someone to devour.

The picture should be coming into focus: God wants to do good in our lives, and Satan wants to destroy our lives. There is a real battle in the spiritual realm, and it's directly impacting you and me.

God calls us to trust Him enough to come to Him in faith, to obey His commands, to rest in His love, and to experience His goodness and power. Satan, on the other hand, is scheming and plotting and deceiving in an all out effort to keep us from having all that God wants to give us.

So what do we do? Are we hopeless? Absolutely not! We are given the very answer in 1 Peter 5:8–10.

> Be of sober spirit, be on the alert. Your adversary, the devil, prowls around like a roaring lion, seeking someone to devour. But resist him, firm in your faith, knowing that the same experiences of suffering are being accomplished by your brethren who are in the world. After you have suffered for a little while, the God of grace, who called you to His eternal glory in Christ, will Himself perfect, confirm, strengthen, and establish you.

Did you see it? We don't have to run and hide at the thought of the devil's rampage. Instead, we are to stand firm in faith. In other words, we can resist Satan by trusting fully in the promises of God.

We Have an Enemy

Yes, we must be "of sober spirit" and be "on the alert." This means we should not take this battle lightly, and we should always be on guard, knowing the devil will try to deceive and destroy. He lies, he schemes, and he deceives, so we should never let our guard down.

But, if we will resist the temptations and keep our eyes focused on the promises of God, then we will overcome. We must learn to recognize the battle and take real action! Flee from Satan, and seek God.

This is the very same principle that changed my life, the truth I discovered in 2 Timothy 2:20–22.

> In a large house there are not only gold and silver vessels, but also vessels of wood and of earthenware, and some to honor and some to dishonor. Therefore, if anyone cleanses himself from these things, he will be a vessel of honor, sanctified, useful to the Master, prepared for every good work. Now flee from youthful lusts and pursue righteousness, faith, love and peace, with those who call on the lord from a pure heart.

If we hope to be vessels of honor, then we must resist the schemes and deceptions of the enemy. Satan will try to lure us away from commitment to godly living and good works. The devil will try to keep our attention focused on ourselves and our wants and needs. He is fully aware of our weaknesses and will not hesitate to take advantage of them.

We must resist him. We must not allow his evil ways to draw us from our true and fruitful purpose in Christ, the purpose of our salvation: bearing fruit.

As we flee from sin and selfishness, and in their place pursue righteousness, faith, love, and peace, we will find victory and freedom. It is then that we will begin to see the fruit start to bud in our lives. If we endure and continue to surrender our wills to the God of heaven and earth, we will reap amazing joy, peace, and eternal rewards. This is God's will for you and me.

Please examine your life and ask yourself if you can identify an area or two where the devil is attacking you. You may also talk with someone close to you, someone you trust will be honest with you, so they can help you to identify your weaknesses or places in your life where you are susceptible to the enemy. Awareness is essential in your fight to resist the evil one. You need to know where you are most vulnerable so you can learn how to flee from his wicked schemes.

Once you have identified the places where you need fortification, begin to replace old and risky habits with new and godly ones. Put into practice the things you have learned and begin to walk in the newness of life, doing so *will* change your life!

❊ ❊ ❊

The Word

I thank God regularly for the Bible. I know it has the power to conform and transform our lives. God has given us His testimony about life and instructions as to how we are to live. This is well expressed in 2 Timothy 3:16–17.

> "All Scripture is inspired by God and profitable for teaching, for reproof, for correction, for training in righteousness; so that the man of God may be adequate, equipped for every good work."

We must have faith in God's ability to tell us what we need to know. If we believe He is the Creator of heaven and earth, can we not believe He is able to inspire men to write His words? This is what 2 Peter 1:20–21 claims to be true.

> But know this first of all, that no prophecy of Scripture is a matter of one's own interpretation, for no prophecy was ever made by an act of human will, but men moved by the Holy Spirit spoke from God.

If we will conform our lives to the word of God, our lives will begin to change. God, who is the Author, Designer, Creator, and Sustainer of life, has given us His instructions and testimony. His words are absolutely true and trustworthy; they are indeed the keys to joy, peace, and freedom. John 8:31–32 puts it this way.

> So Jesus was saying to those Jews who had believed Him, "If you continue in My word, then you are truly disciples of Mine; and you will know the truth, and the truth will make you free."

Our actions are based on our inner thoughts. Our beliefs about life and eternity directly shape who we are and what we do. If we want to be godly, then our beliefs must be based on God's truth and not our own ideas or imaginations.

The more we are transformed by God's truth, the more our lives will be changed and conformed into the likeness of Jesus. We all have mixed up and wrong ideas, which are caused by various things. Those misconceptions and misunderstandings of the truth hold us captive and cause us to make ungodly choices. They can also rob us of joy, power, peace, and victory over sin.

So, we must allow God's truth to penetrate deep into our being, down to the very core of who we are. Romans 12:2 states this well.

> And do not be conformed to this world, but be transformed by the renewing of your mind, so that you may prove what the will of God is, that which is good and acceptable and perfect.

We live and act upon our beliefs and innermost thoughts. If these driving forces are based on false information or wrong ideals, then our lives and actions will reflect it. However, if our thoughts and beliefs are godly and true, then our lives will reflect that as well. Our actions are always a direct result of our beliefs.

If we hope to fulfill the Two Greatest Commandments, then we must allow God's truth to transform us from within. As His truth confronts and replaces fallacy and misunderstandings, our lives will be reshaped and begin to look more and more like the lives that Jesus died to give us.

If you want to be a vessel of honor, it will not happen apart from letting God's truth penetrate and transform your mind. His word is able to enlighten us, give us direction, help us avoid sin, and inspire us to love others. The Bible truly is a "lamp unto our feet."

I love Psalm 119:9–11 and 119:105. These passages have directed me and encouraged me many times.

> How can a young man keep his way pure? By keeping it according to Your word. With all my heart I have sought You; do not let me wander from Your commandments. Your word I have treasured in my heart, that I may not sin against You.

> You word is a lamp unto my feet and light to my path.

God has blessed us with truth. He has given us the Bible to help us fulfill the purpose for which we were created. When we let the truth become a guide and help to us, we will find freedom, victory, and joy.

But, like a lantern or flashlight, it will be of no use to us if we do not take it with us and let it light our path. The word is intended to be used; it is meant to enlighten our hearts and minds as we walk through this world. Yet, it cannot do so if we fail to utilize it as God intended. In order to be empowered by the Bible, we need to: read the truth, hear the truth, believe the truth, speak the truth, and obey the truth.

I personally have a list of scriptures taped inside the front cover of my Bible. I call the list "my lamp" because it truly is a "lamp unto my feet and light unto my path." Each verse or passage has been selected because it has guided me, encouraged me, taught me a valuable lesson, or helped me to make a wise choice. Every day I read one of those scriptures, I then think about what it means to me, meditate upon what I think God is trying to teach me through it, and I can often recall how it has changed my life. The next day I will do the same thing with the subsequent scripture. I go down the list and repeat the process each month. Occasionally, I will come across another powerful truth and will add it to my list; I am currently up to thirty-six.

I know this good habit has had a powerful impact upon me. I know that God is using the Bible to change my life in a real way.

I want to encourage you to find scriptures that speak to *your* heart and guide *your* steps. Get to know the promises and warnings of God's word. Meditate on and memorize those verses that have an impact on *your* thoughts and attitudes. Then, and only then, the Bible will become a lamp unto *your* feet.

※ ※ ※

The Holy Spirit

One of the most fundamental truths in Christianity is that of the Trinity: One God who exists in three persons: God the Father, God the Son, God the Holy Spirit. The most common reference to the Trinity is found in Matthew 28:19.

> Go therefore and make disciples of all the nations, baptizing them in the name of the Father and the Son and the Holy Spirit.

We often acknowledge and worship God the Father. We confess Jesus as Lord and exalt Him and praise Him and worship Him, too, but do we worship the Holy Spirit? Are we ignoring one third of the Trinity? Are we neglecting 33 percent of who God is?

The Spirit of God is mentioned for the first time in the Bible in Genesis 1:2, and we find references about the Holy Spirit throughout the Bible, the last time being in Revelation 22:17. The Holy Spirit is mentioned over one hundred times by various names in the New Testament alone.

Yet, I do not remember ever hearing a message preached about the role or significance of the Holy Spirit when I was growing up. In fact, I believe I was almost thirty years old before I ever really learned about this personhood of God. Therefore, I can relate to the people who are mentioned in Acts 19:1–2.

> It happened that while Apollos was at Corinth, Paul passed through the upper country and came to Ephesus, and found some disciples. He said to them, "Did you receive the Holy Spirit when you believed?" and they said to him, "No, we have not even heard whether there is a Holy Spirit."

Yes, I had heard about the *Holy Ghost* but only as a side note, or even in a derogatory way. It was as if people were afraid to mention the indwelling Spirit of God, which is given to every believer, according to Ephesians 1:13-14.

> In Him, you also, after listening to the message of truth, the gospel of your salvation—having also believed, you were sealed in Him with the Holy Spirit of promise, who is given as a pledge of our inheritance, with a view to the redemption of God's own possession, to the praise of His glory.

Titus 3:5-7 also gives us this same message.

> He saved us, not on the basis of deeds which we have done in righteousness, but according to His mercy, by the washing of regeneration and renewing by the Holy Spirit, whom He poured out upon us richly through Jesus Christ our Savior, so that being justified by His grace we would be made heirs according to the hope of eternal life.

For so long I heard about God the Father and Jesus the Son, and I was growing in knowledge and faith, but with so little teaching about the Holy Spirit, I was missing out and lacking more complete truth.

The Holy Spirit

But, now, I know the Holy Spirit is real and that He indwells those who call upon the name of the Lord Jesus Christ. The Holy Spirit comforts, encourages, convicts, and directs us. As John 14:16-17 put it, He is our Helper.

> I will ask the Father, and He will give you another Helper, that He may be with you forever; that is the Spirit of truth, whom the world cannot receive, because it does not see Him or know Him, but you know Him because He abides with you and will be in you.

The promise of the Spirit was made to all who trust in Jesus as their Lord and Savior. We know this based on Acts 3:36-39.

> Therefore let all Israel be assured of this: God has made this Jesus, whom you crucified, both Lord and Christ. When the people heard this, they were cut to the heart and said to Peter and the other apostles, "Brothers, what shall we do?" Peter replied, "Repent and be baptized, every one of you, in the name of Jesus Christ for the forgiveness of your sins. And you will receive the gift of the Holy Spirit. The promise is for you and your children and for all who are far off-- for all whom the Lord our God will call. (NIV)

If you are a Christian, then God's Spirit lives within you. This gives Him access to your innermost being. He can then intercede on your behalf and help you in amazing ways. The Spirit within is powerful, liberating, and life changing. With His help, all things are possible—even breaking way from lifelong habits!

If you want to change, it must come from within. It must be by surrendering your inner self to God's word and His Holy Spirit's guidance. Remember, our actions always follow our beliefs. As we give God access to our hearts, He is able to influence and direct us, and as we cooperate with the Spirit, our lives begin to reflect the character of God.

It is so important to believe in the fact that God's Spirit lives within you if you are a believer. Without faith in the indwelling Spirit, it is impossible to follow Him consistently and to depend on His help.

Please do not ignore the truth about the Holy Spirit. Jesus promised to send a Helper and to empower those who call upon His name.

The Lord does not save us and then leave us alone. He does not expect us to simply figure life out for ourselves and then hold us accountable for our shortcomings. No, God is good and merciful. He has not only offered to forgive us of our sins and give us the hope of eternal life, but He has also provided for our needs as we try to walk in Christian purity and good works. God has given us both the Bible and the Holy Spirit to transform us and guide us from within.

As we walk as believers in this world, we must not ignore the significance of the Holy Spirit. We need His help as we try to live out the commands of God. God has testified and given us the information we need to come to know Him and to mature in our faith.

If you are unfamiliar with the Spirit or if you have been led to believe that the Spirit of God is no longer active in the lives of Christians, I encourage you to spend some time studying upon the matter. The promise of the Spirit was given to *all* believers; please do not let the significance of this truth go un-noticed. He is alive and well, and He is currently working within those who know Christ as their Savior.

❈ ❈ ❈

The Truth About Sin

One of the greatest revelations I have received from the word and Spirit has to do with the reality of sin. As an immature believer, I used to see sin simply as breaking a rule. I knew there were some possible negative consequences, but like a rebellious teenager, I never really thought much about the real significance of my sinful choices. However, by God's grace, He has helped me to see things differently.

When we accept Jesus as our Savior, we are pronouncing Him to be the Lord of our lives; we are submitting ourselves to His Lordship and are therefore putting ourselves under His authority. When we become a Christian, we declare Him the King to whom we will be loyal. Oftentimes, we quote Romans 10:9 because of its implications surrounding salvation by grace, but do we see the full picture?

> That if you confess with your mouth Jesus as Lord, and believe in your heart that God raised Him from the dead, you will be saved.

You see, we cannot be saved without declaring Jesus as our Lord. This does not simply mean we are saying we want to be forgiven and receive the grace that is freely given to us; this is saying we will bow to Him alone as our King.

This is a wonderful thing, and we certainly love to call upon our King during our times of need, but are we truly loyal to Him? Do we honor Him as our Lord?

God has recently opened my eyes and helped me to see that every time I sin, I am not just merely breaking a law or moral standard; I am truly violating His Lordship over me. I am rebelling; I am a traitor. And, according to Matthew 6:24, we cannot serve both God and someone else.

> No one can serve two masters; for either he will hate one and love the other, or he will be devoted to one and despise the other. You cannot serve God and wealth.

This verse does specifically identify wealth as the other master in this case, but we could insert anything in its place: sex, fame, religion, power, or whatever might claim our loyalty.

To be sure, we can only bow down to one lord at a time. We are foolish to think that we can somehow divide our loyalties and affections between two opposing sides. Romans 6:16 helps us to see this truth.

> Do you not know that when you present yourselves to someone as slaves for obedience, you are slaves of the one whom you obey, either of sin resulting in death, or of obedience resulting in righteousness?

Can you see that if we give ourselves to a sinful pleasure, or to telling a lie, or to greed, we are indeed obeying *it* as our master? We cannot be loyal to God while we are obeying something that is in opposition to the character or commands of God. We, therefore, deny His Lordship by submitting ourselves to another. That is treason against our loving and faithful King.

David found out just how God feels about sin. When the king committed adultery and murder, he was confronted by Nathan, a prophet of God, as we see in 2 Samuel 12:9 –10.

> Why have you despised the word of the Lord by doing evil in His sight? You have struck down Uriah the Hittite with the sword, have taken his wife to be your wife, and have killed him with the sword of the sons of Ammon. Now therefore, the sword shall never depart from your house, because you have despised Me and have taken the wife of Uriah the Hittite to be your wife.

When we commit sin, we are *despising* God and His word. When we choose to obey our own lust and desires, we are showing contempt and disregard to our loving Father, who sent His Son to save us. Truly, this is offensive and hurtful to Him.

We can also look at this from another angle. The Bible often refers to the church as the "bride" of Christ. This image is seen often in the New Testament. In Ephesians 5:22–24 we are given this illustration in a very vivid way.

> Wives, be subject to your own husbands, as to the Lord. For the husband is the head of the wife, as Christ also the head of the church, He Himself being the Savior of the body. But as the church is subject to Christ, so also the wives ought to be to their husbands in everything.

Romans 7:1–4 gives us another picture of our "marriage" to Christ.

> Or do you not know, brethren (for I am speaking to those who know the law), that the law has jurisdiction over a person as long as he lives? For the married woman is bound by law to her husband while he is living; but if her husband dies, she is released from the law concerning the husband. So then, if while her husband is living she is joined to another man, she shall be called an adulteress; but if her husband dies, she is free from the law, so that she is not an adulteress though she is joined to another man. Therefore, my brethren, you also were made to die to the Law through the body of Christ, so that you might be joined to another, to Him who was raised from the dead, in order that we might bear fruit for God.

If you have died to the law (Mosaic Law) by receiving Jesus as Lord, then you have been joined to Him as a wife is joined to a husband. You are His, and your vow to make Him yours is binding, just as a marriage vow is binding in the eyes of God.

Also, notice we are told within this passage that we have been joined with Christ so we will bear fruit for God, just as we have seen in so many other passages. But, when we are unfaithful to Christ and give ourselves to another, we will instead bear the fruit of the one we have given ourselves to; our offspring will be sinful deeds instead of godly works.

If we "join ourselves to another," then we are, in a sense, committing adultery against Christ. James 4:4 makes this perfectly clear.

> You adulteress, do you not know that friendship with the world is hostility toward God? Therefore whoever wishes to be friends of the world makes himself an enemy of God.

The Truth About Sin

The message is clear. If we decide to give ourselves to ungodliness of any sort, we are indeed breaking that sacred vow that we have made to join with Christ. This is serious! In fact, this verse shows us that if we give ourselves to sin, we are making ourselves to be enemies of God! After all, if I were to give myself to another woman, wouldn't that make me an enemy of my wife, and wouldn't it cause great damage within my marriage? Is this any less true for my relationship with Christ?

These truths have reshaped my view of sin. I no longer look at committing a sin as unimportant or insignificant. I have a deeper understanding of the implications and the problems that sin causes in my fellowship with God. Treason is a serious offense in any kingdom. Adultery is painful and destroys many marriages; so too, sin, in any form, is very serious, and it causes great harms in the life of a Christian.

If you want to live in victory and strength, you must learn to look at sin in the light of scripture. You must decide just how serious you are going to be in your fight to break free. If you think that committing a sin has no real impact upon your relationship with God, I beg you to think again.

The Lord is very clear in the Bible as to how He feels about sin. Please spend some time reflecting upon the thoughts I have shared and the scriptures I have quoted, and then pray and ask God to help you see clearly in regards to your own fight with sin. He will guide you to truth.

※ ※ ※

Deceived

Satan is a deceiver. That is the way he works, and he is quite proficient: a little white lie here and there; a gentle twist of the truth; a well-laid plan, which leads step-by-step to destruction.

Adam and Eve found out the hard way that the devil is a deceiver. Genesis 3:1–7 help us to see how he led them into his deadly trap.

> Now the serpent was more crafty than any of the wild animals the Lord God had made. He said to the woman, "Did God really say, 'You must not eat from any tree in the garden'? The woman said to the serpent, "We may eat fruit from the trees in the garden, but God did say, 'You must not eat fruit from the tree that is in the middle of the garden, and you must not touch it, or you will die.'" "You will not surely die," the serpent said to the woman. "For God knows that when you eat of it your eyes will be opened, and you will be like God, knowing good and evil." When the woman saw that the fruit of the tree was good for food and pleasing to the eye, and also desirable for gaining wisdom, she took some and ate it. She also gave some to her husband, who was with her, and he ate it. Then the eyes of both of them were opened, and they realized they were naked; so they sewed fig leaves together and made coverings for themselves. (NIV)

Satan is indeed sneaky. After all, Adam and Eve probably would have run for cover had the devil blatantly asked them to sin against God. No, that would have never worked, for the two love birds would have probably recognized the danger and rejected the offer, but as it was, they stepped into the snare, and the rest is history.

Recently, God has helped me to see Satan is still in the deception business. He is still scheming and conniving, and he wants to lead us away from the blessings of God and into a prison of despair, shame, and guilt.

God has helped me to see that all Satan had to do in the garden was to place a small morsel in front of Adam and Eve. He simply made them wonder if perhaps there was something better out there, something worth crossing the boundary that God had placed in their lives for their good.

The trickery was subtle but oh so dangerous. Adam and Eve lived in perfection: fellowship with God, peace, unity, and harmony between husband and wife, all of their needs were met, and they enjoyed their labors. Life was good; they had life to the very fullest, but the Deceiver made them think they were missing out. He dangled the carrot of desire before them, and they took the bait.

I find Satan and his dark forces still use the same tricks of deception. I know there are times when I look past what God has blessed me with and begin to long for something a little better, a little more exciting, a little more satisfying, and I wonder if perhaps I am somehow missing out on what I could have.

Don't we see this in the way Satan tempted Jesus, too? Luke 4:1–13 helps us to see the way in which the devil works.

Jesus, full of the Holy Spirit, returned from the Jordan and was led by the Spirit in the desert, where for forty days he was tempted by the devil. He ate nothing during those days, and at the end of them he was hungry. The devil said to him, "If you are the Son of God, tell this stone to become bread." Jesus answered, "It is written: 'Man does not live on bread alone.'" The devil led him up to a high place and showed him in an instant all the kingdoms of the world. And he said to him, "I will give you all their authority and splendor, for it has been given to me, and I can give it to anyone I want to. So if you worship me, it will all be yours." Jesus answered, "It is written: 'Worship the Lord your God and serve him only.'" The devil led him to Jerusalem and had him stand on the highest point of the temple. "If you are the Son of God," he said, "throw yourself down from here. For it is written: "'He will command his angels concerning you to guard you carefully; they will lift you up in their hands, so that you will not strike your foot against a stone.'" Jesus answered, "It says: 'Do not put the Lord your God to the test.'" When the devil had finished all this tempting, he left him until an opportune time. (NIV)

Satan promised to give Jesus what He physically wanted, emotionally wanted, and what He was going to eventually have anyway. The enemy knew Jesus' weakness just as he knows ours. The devil tried to deceive Jesus by twisting the promises of God into half-truths. He tempted Jesus in the same ways in which he tempts us, according to Hebrews 4:15.

> For we do not have a high priest who cannot sympathize with our weaknesses, but One who has been tempted in all things as we are, yet without sin.

Jesus was tempted by the devil, just as we are tempted. Jesus was a man, so He was susceptible to Satan's schemes, too, yet He never gave in to the tempter. Jesus could not be deceived.

Promises, promises, promises . . . the devil makes us all kinds of promises but is never able to deliver. Satan wants us to think more money will make us happier and help us feel more secure. He wants us to believe there is more fun and pleasure in immoral sex rather than within the boundaries of marriage. The devil plants seeds of doubt, causing us to believe that our current relationship with God is not really enough and that we are somehow falling short. The enemy sets these traps by whispering in our ear that we are missing out.

Don't be deceived. Stand firm in your faith and resist the lies. God will help you to recognize the devil's plots and create a path of escape.

The best way I know to deal with deception is to reinforce truth. We can more easily spot lies when we are familiar with facts. And we will be more able to identify and reject the devil's cunning schemes when we are well acquainted with God's word. I know this is true because I have experienced it in my own life.

If you do not have a regular devotional or Bible reading time in your life, I encourage you to work at developing this invaluable habit. You do not have to be a Bible scholar, and you do not have to spend hours at a time reading scripture. But if you will invest a little time each day in getting to know God's word and memorizing verses that empower you, your life will be greatly impacted, and you will gain wisdom and insight, which will help you avoid the snares of deception and half-truth.

Jesus resisted temptation and avoided sin by knowing and quoting the word of God. So can you.

✤ ✤ ✤

Freedom

One thing I had to learn after salvation was the fact I am not perfect in my actions or thoughts, but that I am perfect in righteousness. This is a complicated and difficult thing to understand with our weak human minds, but it is nonetheless true and vitally important.

The New Testament clearly teaches us we are saved by grace and that we are instantly made righteous and holy in the sight of God once we receive Jesus as our Lord and Savior. Titus 3:5–7 reminds us it is the work of God within us that qualifies us as holy and righteous, it is not our own goodness.

> He saved us, not on the basis of deeds which we have done in righteousness, but according to His mercy, by the washing of regeneration and renewing by the Holy Spirit, whom He poured out upon us richly through Jesus Christ our Savior, so that being justified by His grace we would be made heirs according to the hope of eternal life.

And Galatians 2:20–21 explains that it is Christ within us that qualifies us as acceptable to God. Here, we are also taught that if following religious rules or if doing good deeds makes us righteous, then Jesus died for nothing.

> I have been crucified with Christ; and it is no longer I who live, but Christ lives in me; and the life which I now live in the flesh I live by faith in the Son of God, who loved me and gave Himself up for me. I do not nullify the grace of God, for if righteousness comes through the Law, then Christ died needlessly.

Most evangelical Christians today will give an approving nod to salvation by grace but then teach and preach religion and legalism as a means of Christian living. For example, I have talked with Christians who believe we can do nothing to save ourselves, but then turn around and say that a person has to stop sinning to go to heaven. That simply doesn't make sense, and it is not Biblical.

This is a shame, since the Bible clearly teaches that we are not saved by our actions or by our works. Ephesians 2:8-9 should put this to rest.

> For by grace you have been saved through faith; and that not of yourselves, it is the gift of God; not as a result of works, so that no one may boast.

Can you see that we are absolutely saved by faith? If so, don't stop there, that same faith continues to allow us to be holy and righteous in the eyes of God, even when our actions and attitudes are anything but holy and righteous?

We are fallible. We are weak. We are human.

God knows this and allows for our errors and imperfections by enabling us to remain saved and in relationship with Him because of Jesus. As we have already seen, we are not saved by performing religious activities or by being good people, and we do not remain saved by doing good works or by adhering to certain spiritual practices. Instead, we remain in the grace freely offered to us by God through faith in Jesus. Without this truth, we would be hopeless and could never remain in good standing before God.

Yet, we often fear that we might somehow fall from grace or lose our salvation due to our failures. We also strive and labor in hopes of showing God that we *truly* do believe. All the while, we claim salvation by grace. This makes us very susceptible to the bondage of laws and traditions of men.

Paul found the same kind of misunderstanding and confusion among some of the first generation of believers. The Galatians gladly received the gospel but were then held captive by religious leaders who taught rules and regulations. This is evident in Galatians 3:1-3.

> "You foolish Galatians, who has bewitched you, before whose eyes Jesus Christ was publicly portrayed as crucified? This is the only thing I want to find out from you: did you receive the Spirit by the works of the Law, or by hearing with faith? Are you so foolish? Having begun by the Spirit, are you now being perfected by the flesh?"

The Galatians received salvation by believing in Jesus, just as we do. They realized they could not save themselves, so they trusted in the grace of God. Yet, the Galatians fell back into legalism. They understood that they were saved by grace but were then somehow deceived into believing they had to maintain their salvation by works of religion.

The Galatians were led astray by false teaching and found themselves bound up by rules and religious ceremonies.

Today, some well-meaning believers teach that people who are saved should want to go to church all the time or they should never have the urge to sin. Others claim that you must be able to speak in tongues if you are truly saved. Still others demand that you be fully immersed in water in order to be a real Christian. All of these things may sound good, but they simply are not true. These kinds of teachings and misunderstandings open up the door for legalism and condemnation.

I must confess I personally find it hard to avoid legalism. It is so very easy to expect everyone to like what I like, think the way I think, and deal with problems the way I deal with problems. When others do not meet my expectations, I can quickly begin to feel superior to them or try to convince them that they are wrong and I am right. On the other hand, I may look at them and doubt my own faith or relationship with God based upon how I compare myself to their spiritual gifts, abilities, or appearances of holiness. Either way legalism is nothing more than bondage.

Jesus did not die to place us back under the Law of Moses. He died to set us free so we could live in freedom—in grace. Isn't that the point of the gospel? Isn't that what Paul teaches us throughout the New Testament? Isn't that the message of Galatians 5:1?

> It was for freedom that Christ set us free; therefore keep standing firm and do not be subject again to a yoke of slavery.

You may be wondering what Paul meant when he wrote of a yoke of slavery. We can find out by reading Acts 15:1–2, 6–11.

> Some men came down from Judea and began teaching the brethren, "Unless you are circumcised according to the custom of Moses, you cannot be saved." And when Paul and Barnabas had great dissensions and debate with them, the brethren determined that Paul and Barnabas and some others of them should go up to Jerusalem to the apostles and elders concerning this issue...

> The apostles and the elders came together to look into this matter. After there and been much debate, Peter stood up and said to them, "Brethren, you know that in the early days God made a choice among you, that by my mouth the Gentiles would hear the word of the gospel and believe. And God, who knows the heart, testified to them giving them the Holy Spirit, just as He also did in us; and He made no distinction between us and them, cleansing their hearts by faith. Now therefore why do you put God to the test by placing upon the neck of the disciples a yoke which neither our fathers nor we have been able to bear? But we believe that we are saved through the grace of the Lord Jesus, in the same way as they also are."

The issue which was so upsetting to Paul, Barnabas, and Peter was the teaching that all people must observe the Jewish customs, ceremonies, and laws in order to be Christians. But, as Paul stated, no one was able to live up to that standard and those things were not necessary for salvation in the first place.

We are supposed to live in freedom from religious laws and the traditions of men. We are saved by grace, and we live life in Christ by grace. This does not eliminate the commands of Jesus and teachings of the Apostles to live in purity and good works, but it does free us from the bondage of Jewish Law and man-made religion.

Please do not misunderstand me. Gathering together to worship God and study the Bible is good and needful. Likewise, praying, fasting, meditating on scripture, and serving others are all vital to a full and powerful Christian life. Yet, these are not the way to salvation, and they are not intended to be the goal in and of themselves. Therefore, they should not become the focus. Instead, we need to let them be instruments of transformation and love, *not a yoke of slavery*. Our lives as Christians should be enhanced but not dominated and controlled by the spiritual disciplines, church attendance, and sacrificial service.

On another important note, we should never abuse or misuse our liberty, as we are taught in Galatians 5:13-14. At times this can be a real challenge as we learn to walk in grace.

> For you were called to freedom, brethren; only do not turn your freedom into an opportunity for the flesh, but through love serve one another. For the whole Law is fulfilled in one word, in the statement, "YOU SHALL LOVE YOUR NEIGHBOR AS YOURSELF."

Our freedom in Christ is freedom from religion and legalism, but that does not give us the right to do as we please or to cause harm to others. Instead, we should always remember that we will be judged by God based upon our use of the freedom which He has given us. We will be held accountable for the way we lived as Christians; whether or not we used our liberty to love others or merely to serve ourselves? How do I know this? James 2:12 points it out.

> So speak and so act as those who are to be judged by the law of liberty.

Freedom does not come without responsibility or accountability! This is a fact we would be wise to accept and live by. Our liberty in Jesus is great, we are free from the burdens of religion and tradition, but we must be careful as to the use of our liberty. Rejoice in the grace of God and the freedom it brings, but never let God's grace become an excuse for sin.

✤ ✤ ✤

Standing in Grace

As I have stated many times before, I know I was eternally saved when I received Christ at the age of sixteen. I believe fully I was forever forgiven and washed clean the day I received the free gift of grace, which Jesus died to offer me.

Yet, I also know that I continued to act sinfully. I believed in Jesus and I wanted to honor and obey Him, but I constantly failed miserably. This resulted in many different responses. Sometimes, I would tearfully confess my sins to God and beg for mercy. At other times, I would vow to never sin again, and I fully meant it at that moment. And, yes, there were those times when I just flat out didn't give two cents about my faith or the possible results of my actions and, therefore, went headlong into ungodliness.

I lived in torment, fearing the loss of my salvation, even though I kind of thought that wasn't possible. I also heavily questioned the sincerity of my conversion experience, doubting that I had originally had enough faith to be saved; after all, how could a "real Christian" act in such ways?

But, now, I have come to understand I was not only saved by grace, but that same grace continues to keep me saved. This has brought me tremendous relief and has created a much deeper and more meaningful love for God.

The gospel of Jesus Christ does not end at salvation. No, the gospel also applies to our daily lives. Jesus died to save us from eternal damnation, but He has also rescued us from this present evil age. This truth is seen in Galatians 1:3–5.

> Grace to you and peace from God our Father and the Lord Jesus Christ, who gave Himself for our sins so that He might rescue us from this present evil age, according to the will of our God and Father, to whom be the glory forevermore. Amen.

This truth is life-giving. The death and resurrection of Jesus does not only give me the hope of eternal life, but it also takes away every sin that I have committed or will commit since being saved. I have been completely saved from this present evil age! I stand and live in grace. My sins were forgiven once and for all when I received Jesus as Lord and Savior.

How do I know this? Romans 5:1-2 tells me so.

> Therefore, having been justified by faith, we have peace with God through our Lord Jesus Christ, through whom also we have obtained our introduction by faith into this grace in which we stand; and we exult in hope of the glory of God.

These verses show us that we are not only saved by grace, but that same grace continues to cover us. We are born into Christianity by placing our faith in Jesus and are therefore reconciled to God. That reconciliation is not based on our performance but upon the grace of God. That same grace keeps us saved and at peace with God because grace is never based upon our performance! That is verified by Romans 11:6.

> But if it is by grace, it is no longer on the basis of works, otherwise grace is no longer grace.

Is this possible? Was receiving Jesus once enough to ensure that I am eternally secure? If not, what would be enough? Do I have to avoid certain sins or carry out specific religious practices in order to remain saved?

The simple truth of the gospel is that faith in Jesus is enough. Furthermore, the Bible teaches that once we receive Jesus as Lord, we are totally forgiven. In fact, John 5:24 explains this rather well.

> Truly, truly, I say to you, he who hears My word, and believes Him who sent Me, has eternal life, and does not come into judgment, but has passed out of death into life.

This verse teaches us that once we have believed in Jesus, we have moved from death to life and are no longer under the judgment for our sins. At that moment, we are given eternal life. In other words, the deal is done; nothing more is required.

Now, even though we stumble and fall from time to time, we remain children of God, sealed by the Holy Spirit, guaranteed by the work of Christ. I know this is true because of the numerous times this is taught in the New Testament. For instance, 2 Corinthians 1:21–22 and Ephesians 1:13–14 exemplify this reality.

> Now it is God who makes both us and you stand firm in Christ. He anointed us, set his seal of ownership on us,

> and put his Spirit in our hearts as a deposit, guaranteeing what is to come. (NIV)

> In Him, you also, after listening to the message of truth, the gospel of your salvation—having also believed, you were sealed in Him with the Holy Spirit of promise, who is given as a pledge of our inheritance, with a view to the redemption of God's own possessions, to the praise of His glory.

Clearly, the New Testament teaches us that once we have received Jesus as Lord, we have been sealed by the Holy Spirit. This seal is a guarantee or promise of redemption. It is the seal of our son-ship as a believer. It identifies us as born again Christians.

So, now that God's word has put to rest my fears of losing my salvation, I can live in freedom. This does not mean I can live in sin without consequence, but it does mean I do not have to be bound up by tradition and religious rules in an effort to try to maintain my salvation.

Paul had to frequently address this issue because living in grace is so hard for us to understand. We see in Romans 6:1–7 that this new paradigm is difficult to understand and sometimes confusing to live by.

> What shall we say, then? Shall we go on sinning so that grace my increase? By no means! We died to sin; how can we live in it any longer? Or don't you know that all of us who were baptized into Christ Jesus were baptized into his death? We were therefore buried with him through baptism into death in order that, just as Christ

was raised from the dead through the glory of the Father, we too may live a new life. If we have been united with him like this in his death, we will certainly also be united with him in his resurrection. For we know that our old self was crucified with him so that the body of sin might be done away with, that we should no longer be slaves to sin– because anyone who has died has been freed from sin. (NIV)

To live in grace does not give me permission to live in sin. After all, we have been set free from sin, so why would we want to submit ourselves to it again? Yet, if we do stumble and fall, we do not have to fear total rejection and condemnation.

Romans 8:1 helps us to see that once we are in Christ, we are no longer under condemnation.

Therefore there is now no condemnation for those who are in Christ Jesus.

This truth is also given to us in John 3:18.

Whoever believes in him is not condemned, but whoever does not believe stands condemned already because he has not believed in the name of God's one and only Son. (NIV)

When a person places his or her faith in Jesus, he or she is forgiven once and for all. They move from eternal condemnation to standing in grace. They move from eternal damnation to eternal life, and they will remain in this grace forever.

This fact should not be ignored. We are saved by grace, and we live as Christians by grace. We are guaranteed eternal life based not on our behavior; rather, it is completely based on the saving grace and faithfulness of God.

Again, standing in grace does not remove all of the consequences of sin, but it does remove condemnation or judgment for our sins. The Bible very clearly instructs Christians to avoid sin and to choose godliness, yet not for salvation, since our salvation has already been secured by placing our faith in Jesus. Sin still causes pain and destruction, but it will not separate us from the love of God, and it cannot keep us from heaven.

This truth brings me great joy and hope. The longer I live and the more I realize how amazing God's grace is, the more I rejoice in my salvation. It is a glorious thing to know that I am kept secure by His love and faithfulness, not by my own goodness or ability to follow His commands. Growing in this knowledge has not caused me to run head-long into sin as I once feared it would. No, instead, I have become more thankful and appreciative for what He has done for me, and I more fully desire to honor Him and please Him with my life.

I hope you, too, can find joy and freedom in your salvation. I pray you are able to see that once you are born into the family of God through faith in Jesus, you will remain secure based upon God and not your own works or acts of righteousness.

※ ※ ※

Living in Grace

I can only become a vessel of honor by grace. It is God at work in me that makes it possible. It is the Holy Spirit changing me and transforming me that sanctifies me. It is the grace of God that clears away ungodliness and replaces it with holy and righteous thoughts and actions.

Let's look at Galatians 3:1–5 again as a reminder of the significance of grace when it comes to salvation and godly living.

> You foolish Galatians, who has bewitched you, before whose eyes Jesus Christ was publicly portrayed as crucified? This is the only thing I want to find out from you: did you receive the Spirit by the works of the Law, or by hearing with faith? Are you so foolish? Having begun by the Spirit, are you now being perfected by the flesh? Did you suffer so many things in vain- if indeed it was in vain? So then, does He who provides you with the Spirit and works miracles among you, do it by works of the Law, or by hearing with faith?

As we have seen many times before, this passage indicates salvation does not come by works of the Law and neither does perfection. Simply stated, we cannot be made perfect by religious activities. We are not made perfect by following man-made traditions. We are only perfected by the Spirit at work within us.

We need God's grace to help us overcome our bad habits, wrong theologies, and sinful thoughts. It is by His grace that we are transformed and matured.

Paul not only taught this truth, but he had to live by grace as well. Paul reveals how important grace was to him in 1 Corinthians 15:9–10.

> For I am the least of the apostles, and not fit to be called an apostle, because I persecuted the church of God. But by the grace of God I am what I am, and His grace toward me did not prove vain; but I labored even more than all of them, yet not I, but the grace of God with me.

Paul realized he never deserved salvation to begin with, but he could also see everything he accomplished as an apostle of Christ was a direct result of God's grace. Yes, Paul worked and strove to live in purity and good works, but it was truly the grace of God that helped him to do so.

We all have weakness. We are all prone to give into one sin or another. This is the reality in which we live. Therefore, we all need the grace of God to help us face temptations and to love others as God commands.

Paul, like us, had to face the fact that he was human and, consequently, was plagued with weakness toward sin. He was an incredible ambassador for the Lord, but he was not superhuman. We can see this in 2 Corinthians 12:7–10.

> Because of the surpassing greatness of the revelations, for this reason, to keep me from exalting myself, there was given me a thorn in the flesh, a messenger of Satan to torment me—to keep me from exalting myself! Concerning

this I implored the Lord three times that it might leave me. And He has said to me, "My grace is sufficient for you, for power is perfected in weakness." Most gladly, therefore, I will rather boast about my weakness, so that the power of Christ may dwell in me. Therefore I am well content with weaknesses, with insults, with distress, with persecutions, with difficulties, for Christ's sake; for when I am weak, then I am strong.

Based on this passage, we can assume Paul's weakness must have been pride. He mentioned twice in this passage the thorn in the flesh was intended to keep him from *exalting* himself. Whatever was tormenting him, Paul pleaded with God to have it removed, but the Lord told Paul it was necessary for his good, and His grace would help him through. The Lord also told Paul that in this area of weakness, the Lord's power would become a way of strength to him.

The same promise is made to us: in our weakness, He is strong.

We all have struggles. We all have problems that require God's grace to empower us if we hope to be victorious. It is only by His grace we can overcome and endure. Then, when we overcome, we can only give Him the glory, knowing that it was His grace and power that brought us through.

The simple truth is God wants us to lean on Him and to call upon His name. We are told to seek His help and to depend on His grace. It is just as Hebrews 4:14–16 reveals.

> Therefore, since we have a great high priest who has passed through the heavens, Jesus the Son of God, let us hold fast our confession. For we do not have a high priest who cannot sympathize with our weaknesses, but One who has been tempted in all things as we are, yet without sin. Therefore let us draw near with confidence to the throne of grace, so that we may receive mercy and find grace to help in time of need.

God doesn't want us to ignore our weaknesses and act like we are independently strong and able to walk in purity and good works on our own. No, God wants us to acknowledge our weaknesses and ask Him for help in dealing with those issues in our lives. We are not supposed to cover up our failures and shortcomings; rather, we are to approach the throne of grace and receive the mercy and help He freely offers. When we do, we will know Him more fully, understand His love more completely, and give Him more of our love, attention, and worship in return.

I pray you are able to be honest with God and yourself. There is great freedom in being able to open your heart and pour out your soul before God. Remember, you cannot surprise or shock Him, He already knows who you are, all you have done, and every thought you have ever had. And He loves you anyway!

Please always remember that God's love for you is never based upon your performance; you are loved by Him based upon His love alone, and you are accepted and redeemed based solely upon His grace.

❈ ❈ ❈

The Call

God often times uses the most unusual and seemingly unusable people. Would you have selected Paul to take the gospel to so many and to compose the majority of the New Testament? Our how about Rahab or Jacob or any of the other misfits and scoundrels that God used to change the world?

I must always remember I have been called and equipped to serve by grace. My calling is not based upon who I am, my talents, or in my ability to obey God at every turn in my life. If that were the case, I would have been disqualified long ago. I serve Him by grace alone.

Yet, this is so hard for me to remember; I tend to find myself drifting into legalism regularly. I fight this tendency, but as I mentioned earlier, I seem to have a natural inclination toward rules and holding others to my particular ideals. This causes me great stress at times, and it also causes me to place burdens and standards upon others, which then leads to judging them by my own personal criteria.

I am learning to resist those legalistic tendencies and to replace them with the truth and knowledge of scripture. In my quest to be a vessel of honor, I am learning to listen to the Spirit of Truth and live in the same grace that saved me to begin with.

Becoming a vessel of honor is no small task. It is not easy, yet it is possible. Now that I am aware of the call to be a vessel of honor, and now that I see the difference it will make both in my life and the lives of others, I have set my heart on this lofty goal. And, I am trusting God to help me attain it.

I hope this book has been a help to you. I hope you are able to see just how amazing, wonderful, and merciful our God is, but I also hope you can see how much God wants you to serve Him in purity and through good works.

God has plans for each one of us. He saves us for good works, and He calls us to live in a way that will bring Him glory, honor, and praise. Sin hinders both of these callings and causes so much harm. Those sins cannot take us from the arms of our Savior, but they can prevent us from becoming the person whom God created us to be.

The call is clear: God wants us to be vessels of honor, available to the Master for all good works. This is our responsibility and privilege as sons and daughters of the Most High God.

Satan will try to divert us. He will pick at our weakness and try to deceive us, but we must stand in the power and grace of God. We can resist the devil and flee from sin. As we do, we will find the help and comfort we need. None of us is able to live out the Christian life on our own. We are weak and prone to sin. We need God's help, mercy, and power if we hope to become vessels of honor, and these are freely available to those who will trust in Him and seek His face.

The promises and warnings of God are real. They serve to inspire, encourage, and remind us of the consequences of ungodliness and the rewards of faithfulness. His word is a lamp unto our feet, and the Spirit is our Helper, but we must choose to open our eyes and follow where they lead.

God has created you and saved you for good works. He deeply desires that you bear fruit for His kingdom, and when you do, He will richly reward you. The choice is yours: will you be a vessel of honor?

❖ ❖ ❖

Made in the USA
Lexington, KY
14 May 2011